COMBAT
TECHNIQUES

COMBAT TECHNIQUES

AN ELITE FORCES GUIDE TO MODERN INFANTRY TACTICS

CHRIS McNAB and MARTIN J. DOUGHERTY

THOMAS DUNNE BOOKS

ST. MARTIN'S PRESS ≈ NEW YORK

THOMAS DUNNE BOOKS
An imprint of St. Martin's Press.
All rights reserved.
No part of this book may be used or reproduced
in any manner whatsoever without written permission except in case of
brief quotations embodied in critical articles or reviews. For information,
address St. Martin's Press, 175 Fifth Avenue, New York, N.Y. 10010.

www.thomasdunnebooks.com
www.stmartins.com

Library of Congress Cataloging-in-Publication Data
on file at the Library of Congress

EAN: 0-312-36824-0
ISBN: 978-0-312-36824-1

First U.S. Edition 2007

Editorial and design by
Amber Books Ltd
Bradley's Close
74–77 White Lion Street
London N1 9PF
United Kingdom
www.amberbooks.co.uk

Project editor: Michael Spilling
Design: Brian Rust
Illustrations: Patrick Mulrey and Tony Randell

Printed in Dubai

10 9 8 7 6 5 4 3 2 1

PICTURE CREDITS
BAE Systems: 71
Corbis: 9, 15, 18, 20, 29, 74, 99, 104, 158–159, 160, 162, 167, 171, 181, 184
Getty Images: 13, 37, 62, 63, 67, 84, 93, 115, 117–119, 123, 132, 151, 153, 155 (bottom),
156, 161, 163, 166, 168, 172, 174, 180, 183, 186, 187
Katz: 75
Military Picture Library: 137, 138
PA Photos: 148
TRH Pictures: 38, 39, 47, 70, 73, 82, 95, 98, 109
U.S. Department of Defense: 6, 7, 10–11, 12, 14, 16, 17, 21, 25, 26, 28, 30, 33, 34–35, 36, 41, 42,
45, 50, 52, 56, 60, 61, 65, 68–69, 72, 78, 79, 81, 83, 85, 88–92, 97, 100–101, 103, 105, 106, 111–114, 116, 122,
126–131, 133, 135, 140–147, 149, 150, 152, 154 (top), 157, 164, 165, 170, 173, 177, 185

CONTENTS

INTRODUCTION

Warfare is, at best, an unpleasant and chaotic business. The problem is not that plans do not survive contact with the enemy so much as come apart as soon as they are allowed out of the briefing room.

Plans and planning are useful, and the effects of good command and control at all levels cannot be underestimated. But more often than not it falls to the people on the spot to struggle through whatever is thrown at them and get the job done despite enemy action, logistics and intelligence failures, defective or missing equipment, hunger, thirst, heat, cold, dust, damp, smoke and a multitude of other problems.

The only way overcome these setbacks is to prepare for them. But if their plans fail and their equipment breaks, how can troops be prepared? The answer lies in basic procedures and tactics. Effective combat units must be familiar with all aspects of combat – not just how to march and shoot – and must be able to carry out standard tactical evolutions without detailed instructions.

AN UNFORGIVING ENVIRONMENT

Combat is an unforgiving environment and troops who need to be micromanaged are unlikely to be effective. At the very least, it is important that a commander or officer can rely on his troops to carry out basic tasks without requiring detailed instructions. This is particularly critical when responding to an ambush or 'encounter battle' situation, where there may be a great deal of confusion. The things done in the first few seconds can mean the difference between success and defeat, and, just as importantly, mistakes and missed opportunities can result in heavy casualties.

Combat effectiveness for the individual soldier depends on the application of certain basic skills: marksmanship with weapons and observation techniques to allow an enemy to be spotted and identified; and use of cover and concealment to increase the soldier's chances of survival.

A US soldier participates in a live firing exercise. As well as improving marksmanship, practising with live ammunition is crucial for preparing for real combat situations.

An infantryman from the US 1st Infantry Division takes part in an exercise in woodland terrain. Correct use of cover and concealment is one of the most important skills for an infantryman to master.

However, a combat unit is – or, rather, should be – more than the sum of its parts, and it is here that good training really pays dividends on the battlefield.

A unit that reacts to a situation as a collection of individuals is at a huge disadvantage against an organized force that responds as a unit. If the soldiers know what to do and have confidence in one another, a relatively unskilled unit can defeat a force of more competent marksmen who do not know how to cooperate. Some procedures are practised so often that they become habit. Fire and manoeuvre, flanking movements and the use of smoke grenades to cover an attack or a retreat – good soldiers know how and when to do these things without being told.

As force levels become larger, the options are ever greater. Strong points can be reduced by air or artillery bombardment, or assaulted with the aid of armoured fighting vehicles. Neighbouring units can be called upon for assistance. But this requires good communications and the ability to explain quickly and clearly what is necessary and give an overview of the situation. There is no time in combat for a lengthy and verbose description of the whole situation; the supporting force needs to be told what, where and when.

Communicating with supports is an essential part of combat training.

COOPERATION BETWEEN FORCES
Similarly, larger forces increase the opportunities for costly mistakes and, possibly, disaster. Cooperation between combat arms and indeed between services is of vital importance. Today's soldier does not operate in the traditional 'land, sea, air' environment but in a four-dimensional 'battle space' where the 'fourth dimension' is the electromagnetic spectrum.

Infantry soldiers may fight on the ground but they receive support from low- and high-flying aircraft and missiles, as well as long-range gun, mortar and rocket

Special forces often need to avoid detection by the enemy. One effective method is to split up the party, so that one member of the unit keeps watch from a vantage point while the others remain hidden and camouflaged.

artillery. They use vehicles to get about and to provide fire support as well as to carry weapons capable of dealing with enemy tanks and armoured vehicles. The troops may be landed from naval or riverine units and supported by naval gunfire.

They use electronic signalling equipment, radar and night-vision equipment, while their supporting electronic warfare troops try to deny use of these devices to the enemy. This environment may seem bewildering to the observer. Indeed, it is very difficult for an untrained person to cope in the modern battle space. Yet our soldiers have to do just that, and here again they are assisted by well-practised techniques. A properly trained infantry soldier is not merely able to exist in the modern 'complex battle space' but can make better use of its characteristics than his opponents, thus accruing an advantage that can be used to gain victory.

This book is all about the ways that soldiers do these things. Chapter 1 deals with the very basics – the weapons an infantry soldier uses and how they are properly employed. This chapter examines small arms and hand weapons, all the way up to heavy machine-guns and explosives.

Chapter 2 deals with the basic tactics of the infantry force, including mechanized and airborne operations. Successful infantry forces have evolved these tactics and honed them to a fine art over many years. These techniques and their mastery separate a good infantry force from a group of armed individuals.

Chapter 3 wheels out the big guns: support weapons, including artillery, armour and aircraft, and explains how they fit into the infantryman's battle space. Specialist applications such as anti-aircraft defence are also examined.

Chapter 4 explains how terrain affects infantry combat. Operations in the desert are very different to mountain combat, and the urban environment is the toughest of them all. This chapter deals with the specialist skills and tactical considerations inherent in fighting in different terrain.

Chapter 5 deals with skills and the role of Special Forces. Hostage-rescue, infiltration and reconnaissance are all covered, along with a section on sniping. Recent experience has shown the massive value of the sniper, and the near future may see a huge expansion in this specialist arm.

Chapter 6 concentrates on the most common of modern conflicts: counterinsurgency warfare. Whether dealing with terrorists or an organized revolutionary army, today's infantryman is likely to have to deal with the frustrations and severe dangers of 'war-like situations' where he is restricted by rules of engagement while fighting those who are not. This chapter explains how insurgents operate, how they are tackled and how they can be defeated.

The tactics and techniques detailed in this book are tremendously effective, yet they are nothing without the courage and dedication of the people using them. Let us not forget that at the heart of any successful infantry action is the infantryman himself. It is he who crawls through the mud and returns enemy fire, exposing himself to danger and suffering on behalf of people he may never meet.

In the final analysis, however complex the tools and tactics, we rely on having someone on the spot willing to get the job done. It would appear that Napoleon Bonaparte was right when he said two centuries ago that 'Bravery is never out of fashion'.

Soldiers from the French Foreign Legion's elite Parachute Regiment prepare for a field exercise. They are all armed with sniper rifles and covered with traditional sniper camouflage.

CHAPTER ONE

INFANTRY FIREPOWER

Although the modern infantry unit can draw upon a massive spectrum of firepower – including artillery, armoured support and aerial bombardment – it still needs to possess the fundamental skills of small-arms handling to be effective. Without such skills, the unit will be unable to effect the fire-and-manoeuvre tactics so central to competent war fighting, and it will also jeopardize its own safety should support resources not be available. As recent experience in Iraq and Afghanistan has shown, small-arms engagements still occur with great frequency in low-intensity and counter-insurgency warfare, as well as in open conflict, so personal weapons handling remains at the forefront of military training.

A US soldier on patrol in Mosul, Iraq, scans the street warily, his M4 carbine held at the ready and ammunition pouches strapped across his chest. Note the front grip on his carbine for more stable handling of the weapon.

11

THE FAMILY OF WEAPONS

Military units deploy small arms within certain categories, each category complementing the other in terms of firepower and capabilities. The members of this family are: handguns, submachine-guns, rifles and machine-guns.

In military use, handguns have limited applications. Their low penetrative power, relatively poor accuracy and limited range of around 30m (98ft) make them inadequate weapons in substantial firefights. They are primarily used as backup weapons in case of main weapon failure and as precautionary side arms for situations where security issues are not pressing. Typical examples of modern military handguns are the Beretta Model 92 (the standard side arm of the US Army) and the Glock 17/18, both weapons in 9mm (.35in).

Submachine-guns are, in many ways, the least commonly deployed types of small arm in

NATO troops stop for a communications break during a training exercise. They are armed with a mix of weapons: most have AK assault rifles while one soldier carries the US M16. All the guns are fitted with laser training devices.

military units. The high rate of fire and low-powered pistol rounds used by weapons such as the 9mm Uzi and the 9mm Ingram Mac 10 make them lethal at very close ranges, but wildly inaccurate for aimed fire. However, Special Forces soldiers use high-quality submachine-guns such as Heckler & Koch's MP5 family for urban counter-terrorist operations, where instant heavy firepower is useful. Beyond that, submachine-guns tend to be used in a similar way to pistols as backup weapons, particularly for armoured vehicle crews (the submachine-gun's smaller dimensions ensure that it is easily stowed).

RIFLES

The rifle is the defining small-arms type within infantry units, and each soldier is issued with one as his standard weapon. Most military assault rifles today are either 5.56mm (.21in) firearms such as the US M16A2 and British SA80A2, or 7.62mm (.3in) weapons such as the FN FAL or the infamous AK-47/AKM. (Although even the AK family includes small-calibre rifles such as the 5.45mm AK-74.) Assault rifles command ranges of up to 500m (1640ft), and they provide accurate fire in semi-auto, burst or full-auto modes. By firing rifle cartridges producing muzzle velocities in the region of 1000m/sec (3280ft/sec), rifle rounds offer an increased penetrative capability against commonly encountered structures such as brickwork,

A British soldier in Basra takes aim through the SUSAT sight fitted to his L86A1. The L86A1 is an extended-barrel version of the SA80 assault rifle, and is intended for light support fire.

plasterboard and thin metal plate, and also impart greater kinetic energy to a human target to increase take-down power.

A closer look at the M16A2 illustrates the qualities of the modern assault rifle more fully. The M16A2 is a 5.56mm (.223 Remington) rifle with a length of 100.6cm (39.63in) and a weight (loaded with its 30-round magazine) of some 3.99kg (8.79lb). Apart from the barrel and most of the operating parts, the M16A2 is made mostly of high-impact composite materials, which are extremely durable in field use. In combat, the M16A2 has two fire modes: single-shot or three-round burst. The former is used for

accurate aimed fire at longer ranges, while the latter is used in intense, shorter-range engagements when the soldier needs to put out heavy suppressive fire. To keep the gun controllable in both modes, the M16A2 is fitted with a muzzle compensator, which reduces muzzle flip and also helps shield the muzzle flash from enemy eyes. The sights are of adjustable aperture type, which give respectable aimed fire out to ranges of around 300m (984ft), the standard factory setting for many military rifles.

Beyond rifles such as the M16 are the high-accuracy, long-range rifles issued to snipers. Calibre types for these weapons

Above: A US Marine Corps soldier fires the M2HB .50 calibre machine gun, mounted atop a vehicle, during a mechanized raid training exercise in the Republic of Korea.

Below: A prepared machine-gun position, built for a tripod-mounted GPMG. Note that the extensive sandbag protection does not interfere with the traverse of the machine gun.

vary more significantly, from standard NATO-issue 7.62x51mm (.3x2in) weapons such as the Accuracy International L96A1 and the US M24 Sniper Weapon System (SWS), through to large-calibre rifles such as the .50-calibre Barrett M82A1.

Maximum ranges for these weapons – depending on the ammunition type – extend from around 800m (2624ft) to 2000m+ (6561ft+) for the .50-calibre weapons.

MACHINE-GUNS

At the top of the tree of infantry small arms are machine-guns. Machine-guns are primarily intended for heavy suppressive fire at area targets, and range

from man-portable guns operated by a single individual through to massive, vehicle-mounted weapons. Machine-guns are broken down into three categories: light, medium and heavy machine-guns. Light machine-guns are designed for squad- or fire-team level portability, and today generally utilize the same ammunition types as standard infantry rifles to rationalize unit ammunition usage on the battlefield.

One of the most popular types in use is the FN Minimi, known in US forces as the M249 Squad Automatic Weapon (SAW) and in the British Army as 5.56mm (.21in) Light Machine-gun (LMG).

The Minimi fires the standard 5.56mm round used by many Western assault rifles, including the SA80 and M16, and has a cyclical rate of fire of between 700 and 1000rpm. Although the individual rounds carry no more destructive force than those fired from a standard rifle, such a heavy volume of fire makes the Minimi a powerful battlefield presence.

Medium machine-guns are physically larger weapons that fire full-power cartridges (i.e. rounds that have full-length cases). They are less man-portable and generally require a two-man team for operation. The best examples of this weapon class are the Belgian FN MAG and the US M60, both bipod-mounted (pintle mounts are available for vehicular use), belt-fed 7.62x51mm (.3x2in) guns with rates of fire up to 800rpm (in the case of the FN MAG). Medium machine-guns are used more in sustained-fire roles than light machine-guns; hence they have quick-change barrels to prevent dangerous overheating.

Like medium machine-guns, heavy machine-guns direct devastating fire against area targets, but tend to be used on vehicular mounts because of their great weight. The crowning example of a heavy machine-gun is the .50-calibre Browning M2HB, which can put dropping fire onto a target at ranges in excess of 3000m (9842ft). The reach and destructive force of a heavy machine-gun also categorizes it as an anti-materiel weapon, capable of destroying enemy vehicles, outposts and other structures.

British soldiers train with the Barrett .50 calibre rifle. The Barrett was originally designed as an anti-materiel rifle, but has made anti-personnel kills at over 2400m (7873ft).

The categories of small arms above are the fundamental tools of infantry warfare. In terms of tactical application, the modern soldier should be familiar with them all, and most good training programmes will provide training with the guns outside of the standard assault rifle.

CONTROLLING HANDGUN FIRE

Each individual weapon type has its own fire characteristics and effects. The soldier must master these before he can fully contribute to the power of a fire team.

Regarding handguns, the soldier has to develop a firing technique that maximizes the chances of a hit with what is a fairly inaccurate weapon. (Note here that all techniques relate to automatic handguns – modern soldiers rarely use revolvers.) Grip technique is all important. The firearm is held in the firing hand and the tension increased until the hand begins to tremble. At this point the hand is then relaxed until the trembling disappears – this is now the right grip tension. In terms of aiming hold, the two-handed grip is almost universally taught.

Here the fingers of the non-shooting hand are either wrapped around the fingers of grip hand at the pistol grip, or are cupped beneath the pistol grip to form a 'cup and saucer' grip.

Using the non-firing hand for support stabilizes the gun, reducing both horizontal and vertical movement, and also gives the shooter better body alignment with the target. Using isometric tension between the two hands enhances this stability: the hands pull in opposite directions, creating a tension that improves the rigidity of the hold and braces the arms against recoil.

SIGHTING PROCEDURES

Because handguns are such inaccurate weapons, good sighting procedures are essential for their use. Handgun sights are relatively crude, most having a simple rear notch and corresponding front post. For this reason, handgun training always recommends targeting the very centre of the enemy's torso to maximize the chances of a decisive hit on a vital organ system. For sighted shooting – when there

A US Army colonel practises his combat pistol technique in a Close Quarters Marksmanship (CQM) drill at the Udairi Range Complex, Kuwait. Combat pistol shooting typically does not allow time for considered aim, so more involves 'accurate pointing'.

US Navy personnel train with the Beretta M9 pistol. The two-handed grip is essential to get any sort of accuracy out of a handgun, the aiming point being the centre mass of the target.

is time to take an aim – the front post sight is aimed directly at the centre mass; the rear sight and target will appear hazy, but concentration on the front post will give the best sense of accurate direction. When the target is on, the trigger is squeezed. It is vital that the soldier does not anticipate the gun's recoil, as this often results in dipping the barrel to compensate, which produces low patterns. Of course, combat reality often necessitates that a soldier take shots extremely rapidly without considered aim. In this instance, the soldier should aim the gun instinctively like a pointed finger, directing all his focus at the intended point of impact on the target. Extending the index finger of the support hand along the side of the gun (not along the slide, which would inflict a finger injury as it cycles) aids this process – the soldier simply points at the target with his finger and that is generally where the rounds will go.

VOLUME OF FIRE

In terms of volume of fire, there has been much debate around handgun technique. Many police and military forces have advocated the 'double tap' principle – shoot the enemy twice quickly in the torso to ensure that he goes down. However, combat experience has shown that even being hit by two .45 calibre bullets does not guarantee a takedown. Therefore the 'shoot to stop' principle is now commonly taught. This simply involves putting as many rounds as possible into the assailant in quick succession until circulatory or nervous system shock drives him down to the floor.

A handgun-armed soldier must keep track of how many rounds he has fired. (A modern military handgun such as a Beretta 92 contains 15 rounds of 9mm ammunition.) The soldier should count the rounds used so that he knows when to reload. The best moment to reload is when one round is left in the chamber; that way the gun is immediately ready to fire the moment the fresh magazine is slapped in. (The sensation of recoil is often slightly different when the gun chambers its last round; if the soldier is sensitive to this, he will automatically know when to reload without counting rounds.) Spare magazines are positioned in a pouch or webbing on the support arm side, with the bullets facing forward. This way the soldier can grab another magazine with his support arm without making any awkward twisting movements. As he reaches for a spare magazine, he should press the magazine release with his grip hand to clear out the old magazine. Reloading should take no more than three to four seconds.

SUBMACHINE-GUNS

Submachine-guns are very different to handguns. Soldiers need very disciplined tactics when using these guns because inaccurate heavy volumes of fire are just as much a danger to comrades and civilians as they are to the enemy. An Uzi submachine-gun, for example, will empty its standard 32-round box of 9mm (.32in) ammunition in around three seconds. The two critical elements are recoil and trigger control. Trigger pulls of half a second should be the norm – these each release around seven to eight rounds, and therefore force the soldier to be more disciplined with his aim and also to manage his ammunition consumption better. (With practice, the soldier should be able to fire off single shots with just a flick of the trigger.) Furthermore, full-auto fire tends to produce muzzle climb, so shortening the burst time reduces the risk of shooting high.

In terms of sighting, submachine-guns tend to be close-quarter, rapid-response weapons, so the chances for diligent aim will be minimal. Nevertheless, the soldier should always mount the weapon to the shoulder for firing, with the front sight just held fractionally below the bullseye of the target. The soldier leans forward, his body weight counteracting gun rise during the full-auto burst. Aimed fire is hard to achieve, so often the soldier will literally walk the pattern of bullets onto the target, using observed impacts as a sighting guide. As ammunition consumption is so high, the soldier should – as with handguns – have spare magazines at the ready.

A French Foreign Legionnaire conducts urban training manoeuvres with his sound-suppressed Heckler & Koch MP5 SD6. When firing the SD6 is almost inaudible at over 15m (50ft) distance.

Round-counting is impossible, so in active combat situations the soldier should change magazines based on the number of bursts, switching magazines before his gun is entirely empty.

ASSAULT RIFLE HANDLING

Nothing is more important to a soldier's personal defence than his rifle handling. The central part of rifle-shooting accuracy is the mount. The rifle should be securely controlled by the soldier, and properly aligned between the pocket of the shoulder where the stock sits and the forward hand. Both the trigger hand and forward hand maintain a slight rearward pressure to give the rifle stability in line with the shoulder and a greater control of recoil. A good soldier practises achieving a consistent stock-to-cheek weld, with no head canting and a direct eye alignment along the sights.

Stability is also achieved by the use of external supports. Resting the fore-end on a trench lip, tree branch, wall or any other solid structure reduces the amount of movement in the gun by providing a totally stable front platform and removing much of the muscular tension that results from an unsupported hold. If an external support is not readily available, the soldier can adopt a one-knee position, with the elbow of the forward arm resting on a bent knee. Alternatively, he can lie prone with the elbow of his forward arm supported directly on the ground.

Sighting procedures vary according to the type of sights used. The standard M16A2

US UNIT FIREPOWER – IRAQ

The following is an excerpt from a USMC After-Action Report (AAR) prepared after urban operations in Fallujah, Iraq, in 2005. It shows how squad firepower plays various different roles within an urban assault context:

The squad should be organized by using the traditional three elements of assault, support, and security. The amount of Marines contained within each element will vary according to the squad's number of Marines, the skills and abilities that each individual Marine possesses, and the weapons systems that each Marine employs (M249 SAW, M203, and ACOG scoped M16A4s).

The assault element must contain no SAWs if that is possible. A SAW gunner must never clear rooms. The assault element should contain the most number of Marines because every room must be cleared by at least two *Marines. The support element will supplement the assault by falling in the stack and peeling off to clear rooms. Support should include any engineers or assault man attached to the squad. A SAW gunner should be included in this section in order to provide massive firepower in the house if contact is made. The corpsman is also located in support because he can use his shotgun to breach as well as provide quick medical attention to casualties. The support section will fall in the stack behind the assault element to assist in any way. Security should contain the other remaining SAWs in the squad. The security element is responsible for clearing and securing the courtyard or rooftop foothold prior to the assault element moving to the entry point. When assault and support make entry into the structure, two Marines are left behind to isolate the house (rooftop) and secure the squad's entry point.*

iron sight consists of a rear aperture, through which the soldier can see a framed front post, although various optical sights are available, including the M68 Close Combat Optic and the AN/PAS-13 (V2) and V3 thermal sights for night shooting. The British SA80 is fitted as standard with the Sight Unit Small Arms, Trilux (SUSAT), a 4x optical sight that delivers a superb sight picture and moderate image intensification. However, the SA80 is also fitted with an aperture/post iron sight arrangement for when no SUSAT is fitted, and the SUSAT itself carries an Emergency Battle Sight (EBS) on the top, should the optic fail or be damaged. Here, we will look at the procedures for iron sight control, which forms the fundamentals of all rifle handling.

SIGHT ALIGNMENT

Correct sight alignment is critical – a misalignment of just 2.54mm (0.1in) will result in a target at 300m (984ft) being missed by 1.5m (5ft). The sighting procedure using an aperture sight is as follows. The soldier visually

South Korean soldiers cleaning their weapons. Clean firearms are a fundamental part of military professionalism.

acquires the target and aligns his body in relation to it. He raises the gun to his cheek so that the sighting eye is staring through the aperture, and he aligns the front post with the centre mass of the target. The correct sight picture is formed when the aperture, front post and target are all squarely aligned. The soldier should also attempt to aim keeping both eyes open; this dramatically improves spatial and movement awareness, allowing the soldier to track a dynamic target better.

WIND AND GRAVITY

However, wind and gravity also affect the correlation between sight picture and Point of Impact (POI). If the soldier's gun is zeroed for 300m (984ft), then the sight picture should be raised above the POI for any targets beyond that range. Similarly, a 16km/h (10mph) crosswind will shift a 5.56mm (.21in) round 38cm (10in) from the POI at 300m (984ft), and requires a corresponding adjustment. In professional armies, good training and the use of quality sights will help the soldier adjust to gravity and wind effects. Moving targets also require special sighting procedures. For example, an enemy soldier running at 13km/h (8mph), 90 degrees to the firer, and at 300m (984ft) will cover 1.4m (4.5ft) between the moment of firing and the bullet reaching him. During training, the soldier practises lead calculation based on a wide range of scenarios, and multiplies the body dimensions of the target to give a lead picture. (For an enemy soldier with a body depth of 30.5cm/12in, the firer

LOW-LIGHT SHOOTING

Shooting with standard sights in low-light or night-time conditions requires the special adaptation of standard firing techniques. In these situations, the eyes use different parts of their structure (the rods around the peripheries of the eye rather than the cones in the centre), with an important effect on marksmanship – silhouetted targets lose their silhouette if stared at directly, appearing more clearly in the peripheral vision. This effect is particularly pronounced if the soldier has moved from a light situation to a dark one quite rapidly (such as being flown out to a dark combat zone straight from a brightly lit headquarters).

The best way to counter such night blindness is to give the eyes time to acclimatize before the mission. Soldiers destined for a night operation should spend at least 40 minutes in a very dark room to increase their light sensitivity. During the deployment phase, artificial light use is strictly controlled as even a flashlight can degrade night vision. In terms of shooting, aimed sighting at a target will be difficult – either the sights will not offer good visibility or the target will visually fade. Instead, the soldier should point instinctively at the target while using his peripheral vision, keeping his eyes moving to obtain as much information as possible. Night shooting also produces a tendency to shoot high, so the soldier aims towards the lower portion of the target. He can also use auditory signals to guide his accuracy, cupping a hand behind one ear to give better directional feel. Of course, most modern armies destined for night operations will equip their soldiers with night-vision devices, either as goggles or as weapon sights.

imagines four-and-a-half body widths in front for the running scenario described above.) Crucially, the soldier pulls the trigger while he is moving the gun; if he stops the gun for even a fraction of a second to pull the trigger, it is likely that he will miss behind the target.

BREATH CONTROL

During target acquisition the soldier attempts to control his breathing. For deliberate, aimed shooting, the soldier should breathe normally but pause at the bottom of an out breath to take the shot. Breathing, and holding the breath when the lungs are full, cause either body movement or muscular tension, both of which are transferred into gun movement. By pausing on the out breath, the body is in its most stable state, although the soldier must take the shot within a few seconds before oxygen depletion introduces tremble. For rapid shooting at fleeting targets, however, the soldier usually does not have time to introduce a controlled breathing cycle. Here, he should simply hold his breath just as he is about to pull the trigger.

A US soldier in Iraq in 2004 seen on night patrol. He is using night vision goggles and he has a weapon-mounted torch, which can also serve as a close-range aiming device.

Point fire involves all the soldiers of a squad or similar unit directing their fire onto a single target. The purpose can be either to suppress the enemy or inflict destruction upon the position.

TRIGGER PULL

Trigger pull is the fourth vital ingredient of assault rifle marksmanship. The soldier squeezes the trigger rather than yanking it backwards, which usually results in the gun being knocked out of alignment. The soldier should also avoid tensing his shoulders before the shot; this results in a hunching action that moves the stock and so alters POI.

MALFUNCTIONS

Shooting skills are irrelevant if a gun malfunctions. To ensure reliability, the soldier should always strip and clean his weapon after use, ensuring that all moving parts (particularly gas systems and bolts) are free from propellant deposits and other dirt, and that barrels and chambers are pulled through. The professional soldier also pays close attention to magazines, checking for any damage to the feed lips or weakening of the magazine spring. The gun should be properly oiled but not excessively; too much oil attracts dirt and dust, forming what is in effect a grinding substance around all moving parts.

Soldiers also need to be properly trained in handling weapon malfunctions in the field, something that can have potentially lethal consequences in combat. If a gun jams, the soldier momentarily loses his contribution to the firepower and sector cover of his squad or fire team. He therefore announces the malfunction clearly to his comrades so that they can compensate. Most malfunctions result from cartridge misfeed;

simply operating the bolt handle manually is often enough to clear it. However, more serious malfunctions may require a soldier to field strip his weapon and carry out a basic repair or, more likely in a combat situation, acquire another weapon to carry on the fight. As noted earlier, handguns are often carried specifically for these unwelcome events.

FIRE CLASSIFICATIONS

Before looking at how machineguns are handled, it is useful to understand the classifications of fire used by the military. Within these classifications, there are some critical terms to understand:

DEAD GROUND: the ground within a weapon's range and sector that cannot be hit by fire from that weapon.

CONE OF FIRE: the cone-shaped pattern formed in the air by the flight of multiple bullets fired from a weapon.

BEATEN ZONE: the area where the cone of fire actually contacts the ground.

GRAZING FIRE: fire where the rounds do not climb higher than 1m (3ft 4in) above the ground.

PLUNGING FIRE: fire where the flight of the rounds is higher than a standing man, except in the beaten zone.

With these concepts in mind, small-arms fire is classified by the relationship of fire between both gun and the target. There are four categories: frontal, flanking, oblique and enfilade. Frontal fire is directed straight at the front of the target. Flanking fire runs along the target's flank. With oblique fire, the long axis of the beaten zone (beaten zones tend to create an oval-shaped pattern) is at an offset angle to the long axis of the target. Enfilade fire has the beaten zone's long axis corresponding with the long axis of the target.

Flanking fire and enfilade fire are the most destructive classifications of fire, as they maximize the chances of bullets striking multiple targets within the duration of the burst. Of course, the equation is affected by how many soldiers are shooting at the same time. Fire coordination between soldiers and units is generally governed by two principles: point fire and area fire. As the names suggest, point fire consists of a unit directing all the firepower against a single point, such as an enemy bunker, while area fire sees the combined fire directed long the length of the target, such as a vehicle convoy. All the above concepts are particularly important for the application of machine-gun fire.

Some of the principles of sighting, breath control and trigger pull outlined above for assault rifles apply equally to machine-guns. However, there are some key differences involving machine-gun handling. Apart from light machine-guns such as the SAW, many machine-guns

A proper fighting position should offer multiple angles of fire. Here a two-man trench, with fire zones marked in red, has its oblique fire sectors marked out with sector stakes set in the ground.

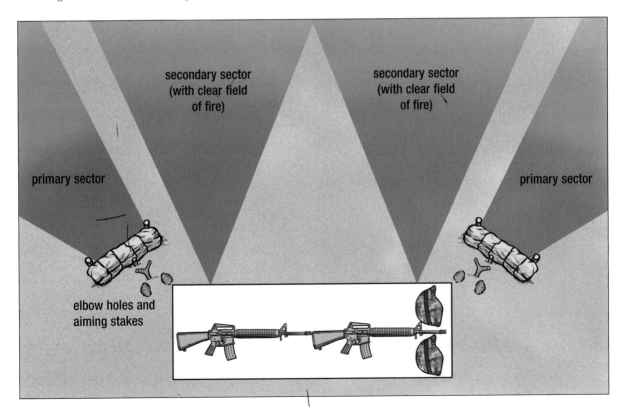

secondary sector
(with clear field
of fire)

secondary sector
(with clear field
of fire)

primary sector

primary sector

elbow holes and
aiming stakes

require crew handling. In US forces, medium and heavy machine-guns tend to be assigned three personnel: a gunner, an assistant gunner, and an ammunition bearer. In turn a leader will direct their actions. The leader will control machine-gun fire through verbal, auditory or hand-signal communications, designating the target and the type of fire required (small-unit fire Standard Operating Procedures is covered in more detail in the next chapter).

When firing a machine-gun, the gun crew must balance

Firing positions can vary, but all should provide maximum cover to the shooter while allowing him freedom to control his weapon and quickly acquire targets.

firepower with the need to keep the barrel cool – too much rapid fire results in the barrel reaching critical temperatures, resulting in jams and even spontaneous firing of rounds (the heat in the chamber is sufficient to set off a round). In sustained-fire modes, the crew will fire bursts of up to nine rounds, leaving four to five seconds between each burst to promote barrel cooling. If this rate is maintained, the barrel will need changing after about 10 minutes. For rapid fire, 10–12 round bursts are separated by only two to three seconds, with a barrel change after two minutes, and during cyclical fire – when belts of ammunition are run through with no pauses – the barrel needs changing after only 60 seconds.

In terms of aim, the machine-gun crew relies much more on the observed impact of rounds to guide them to the intended POI. Typically, the machine-gun is sighted at the target and a short burst is fired. The crew observes the impacts, and then makes either a sight adjustment or adjusts the alignment of the gun. Tracer bullets aid this process. In standard usage, a tracer bullet occurs once for every three or four rounds of standard ball ammunition in the machine-gun belt, providing a visual guidance to fire. Tracers, however, drop more quickly than ball rounds (they lose mass as the incendiary component burns outs), so the machine-gunner must not base all his aim on tracer flight.

A member of the 173rd Airborne Brigade mans a defensive fighting position on the streets of Al Hawijah during Operation Iraqi Freedom. He is armed with the M240, the US version of the 7.62mm Belgian FN MAG.

When considering machine-guns, and indeed any type of military small arms, it must always be remembered that each type of weapon has its limitations and strengths, so units combine firepower to cover all their bases, as it were. For example, in the US Army Rangers, a four-man fire team has two soldiers armed with standard M16s, a third soldier with an M203 Grenade Launcher attached to his M16, and a fourth man armed with a SAW. This combination, followed with subtle variations by many other units and armies, allows the fire team to generate a wide number of point, area and covering-fire options. In turn, medium and heavy machine-gun teams provide more extensive fire options at platoon and company level. When a military unit is well trained, it should be able to coordinate its small-arms fire with tremendous effect upon a wide range of targets.

MINES

Mines, while politically controversial, remain extremely useful area denial and attrition weapons. In current US Army terminology there are four basic types of minefield: protective, tactical, nuisance, and phoney. The purpose of a protective minefield is fairly self-explanatory. It serves as a protective frontage or perimeter around a group of soldiers and their positions/equipment. Should an enemy attack, the minefield is intended to: a) alert the soldiers to the attack; b) delay enemy offensive movement; and c) inflict damage on the enemy's men, vehicles and materiel. Protective minefields can be extremely large and deliberately laid to cover, say, all the ground in front of a battalion deployment. Conversely, a single platoon or company might lay a hasty protective minefield in front of temporary static positions (such as a night camp), in which case the unit is also duty-bound to recover the mines before it moves to new positions.

While protective minefields are entirely defensive in nature, tactical minefields have an offensive purpose. Tactical minefields are emplaced to

interfere with an enemy's manoeuvre and attrit his resources. A tactical minefield might be placed along an expected route of travel or at an ambush site. Tactical minefields require the mines to be difficult to detect to have full effect. A nuisance minefield, by contrast, can actually be fairly visible. Its purpose is tactical, but it is intended more to enforce delay and confusion among enemy forces and so deprive them of tactical initiative. A phoney minefield has a similar effect without the application of mines. Instead, ground is disturbed and indications of mine presence

are emplaced without any actual minelaying. Allied troops must enforce strict discipline to keep up the pretence, making sure all vehicles and personnel manoeuvre around the phoney minefield and give it corresponding respect in radio communications.

MINE TECHNOLOGY OPTIONS

In terms of mine technology itself, a modern army has a bewildering array of options. However, the types of mine neatly separate into two categories: anti-tank (AT) and anti-personnel (AP). AP mines are designed to kill or injure enemy soldiers, although they can

A US soldier sets up a Claymore mine around a security position in Afghanistan in 2004. The mine is best used where the terrain channels the enemy into a confined kill zone.

contain enough blast force to wreck a vehicle wheel or even a tank track. There are a massive array of AP mine types – over 700 types are currently listed worldwide – but the most common types are blast mines (buried mines delivering a high-explosive blast), bounding fragmentation mines (throws a canister into the air, which explodes to create an area shrapnel effect) and directional mines (fires out fragments or other missiles in the direction of the enemy). Blast AP mines tend to be specifically designed to incapacitate an enemy rather than kill him. Crude wooden box mines such as the PMD-6 or advanced mines such as the US M14 contain just enough explosive force to wreck a foot, ankle or leg. Bounding fragmentation mines, by contrast, are intended to kill. The US M16 group of mines or the Eastern European OZM-4s fire out ball bearings or steel rods with a lethal radius of 15m (49ft) and a wounding radius of up to 30m (98ft). Directional mines work on a similar principle, but they are emplaced on stakes above the ground instead of being buried

beneath the soil. The two classic directional mine types are the former Soviet MON-50 and the US M18A1 Claymore. When detonated, the latter blasts out 700 metal ball bearings in a 60-degree horizontal arc at a maximum height of 2m (6.5ft), with casualties sustained to range of 100m (328ft). Fragmentation mines can also be emplaced on fixed stakes above the ground to give accurate control over their explosive field. Note that AP mines are generally initiated by three methods: a pull on a trip wire, physical pressure on above-ground prongs or a buried pressure plate, or are command detonated by electrical signal.

AT mines have, true to their purpose, much greater explosive

force. The US M15 AT mine, for example, contains 9.9kg (20.9lb) of Composition B explosive, enough to wreck completely a large armoured vehicle. AT mines tend to rely purely on explosive force for their effects, although mines such as the US M21 have shaped-charge warheads that direct the blast more precisely, resulting in the complete destruction of a vehicle and its occupants.

AT mine initiation mechanisms vary considerably. A pressure fuse is the basic type, and is

Claymore mines can be tripwire operated, here against a path frequented by the enemy. Almost everyone in a 50 degree arc out to 50m (164ft) will be killed.

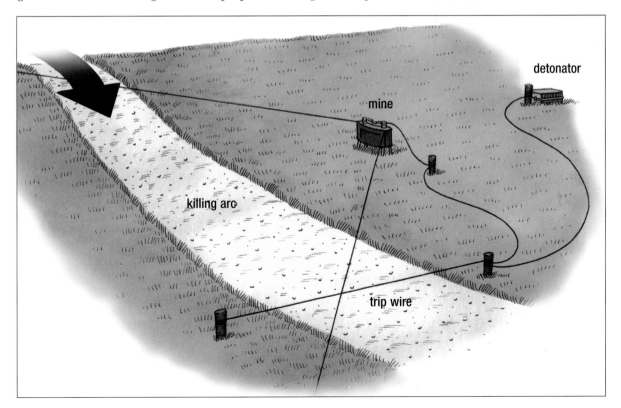

triggered by vehicle weights of more than 100kg (220lb). Proximity fuses detonate the mine by detecting nearby vibrations, acoustic signatures, magnetic fields or electro-magnetic forces characteristic of a passing vehicle. Tilt rod and break wire fuses rely on the enemy vehicle contacting a physical above-ground system that triggers the detonation.

MINE EMPLACEMENT

Mine emplacement, both in terms of patterns and individual emplacement, is a broad and complex topic. There are, however, some general principles. Large protective minefields tend to be laid around either a row formula or a 'standard' pattern. The row formula emplaces mines in regular rows; hence a mine-laying vehicle often puts down this pattern. Mine rows are fast to emplace and, when correctly put down, they leave no easy routes for enemy through-passage, while leaving lanes for safe Allied movement. The standard pattern is more variable and therefore takes more time to place. It consists of various 'strips' and 'clusters' of mines placed together to form a barrier. Note that for a truly effective minefield, a mixture of AT and AP mines are used, such as four AP mines for every one AT mine.

Of course, mapping out and laying a large minefield is extremely time consuming, but there are other options for hasty mine emplacement. There are many different types of scatterable mines – known in US terminology as 'Scatmines'. Scatmines are fired or dropped onto the target area by means of artillery shell, airdropped container or special deployment pack or gun. Once deployed, they sit upon the ground until disturbed by an enemy vehicle or soldier. Scatmines allow extremely rapid minefield deployment, and also allow units to lay minefields remotely and well behind enemy frontlines. A good example of this type of mine is the US

A US engineer searches an uninhabited area of Bagram Air Field for land mines and unexploded ordnance. The rough, rock-strewn and broken soil is ideal for concealing land mines.

Soldiers of the French Foreign Legion train in mine clearance. The clearance procedure also requires much paperwork, informing other units of cleared routes.

Modular Pack Mine System (MOPMS). This is a 74kg (162lb) suitcase-shaped mine dispenser that contains 21 mines (17 AT and four AP). When the unit is command initiated, it fires out the mines to distance of 35m (115ft) in a 180-degree arc. The portability and speed of the MOPMS make it a useful tactical tool, but one, as with all scatterable mines, that must be used with caution. A casual deployment can render an entire area lethal, an area that may need to be used by Allied troops owing to unexpected battlefield developments. For this reason, many Scatmines automatically detonate or deactivate after a short period of time, often around 24 hours.

Emplacing conventional mines by hand takes significant training and understanding to do properly. For buried AT mines activated by pressure plates, the soldier should dig a hole deep enough so that the pressure plate sits about 5cm (2in) below the surface. The earth beneath the mine should be packed solid, preferably using gravel, to ensure that the mine is firmly seated and will not compress. Most crucially, the sides of the hole are dug at a 45-degree angle to the base of the mine. This ensures that if a vehicle runs over the edge of the hole, the pressure of the earth slipping sideward will detonate

the mine – a straight-sided hole will take a vehicle's weight on its vertical sides. If the mine is buried in soft soil, a board or plate can be placed over the top of the hole to increase downward pressure.

Whereas AT pressure plate mines are buried with earth, similar AP mines tend to be placed in a hole and then simply covered with light camouflage. For mines detonated by prongs, tilt rods or tripwires, it is important to provide adequate camouflage for the initiation mechanism. The systems are best

emplaced in ground with a good covering of foliage (in war zones, soldiers will often have a healthy respect for grassy verges that run alongside busy military movement routes, as these are common sights for casual mine emplacement).

There are strict military and international conventions for the marking, recording and reporting of minefields. Even deployment of Scatmines needs to be diligently recorded, with full coordinates provided, and perimeter markings should make clear to civilians that there is a

VARIETIES OF HAND GRENADE

Beyond fragmentation grenades, there are several other types of grenade in widespread use with military forces. These are:

SMOKE GRENADES: used as signalling devices (ground-to-ground or ground-to-air), for marking target or landing zones, or to conceal unit movements.

RIOT CONTROL GRENADES: these are typically filled with an irritant gas – usually CS – and are used for dispersing crowds during riot situations.

INCENDIARY GRENADES: designed to set fire to equipment and buildings, incendiary grenades usually contain a thermite or thermate (a modern version of thermite) compound that burns ferociously.

STUN GRENADES: stun grenades produce an intense bang and flash without the lethal fragmentation patterns of a fragmentation grenade or a killing blast. They are used to disorientate an enemy and provide a diversion for an assault.

CONCUSSION GRENADES: concussion grenades impart a very powerful shockwave but have low fragmentation properties. They will kill and incapacitate enemy soldiers in the immediate vicinity of the detonation, but are of minimal danger to nearby friendly troops.

---

minefield present. Unfortunately for the world, hundreds of thousands of mines have not been marked, and these kill and maim thousands of civilians every year.

GRENADES AND EXPLOSIVES

Although military demolitions are an expert speciality, all infantrymen are familiar with one type of explosive device – the hand grenade. Hand grenades are available in several different formats, the most common combat variety being the fragmentation grenade. For example, the standard US Army fragmentation grenade is the M26 (on which the British L2 is based). The M26 contains 182g (6.5oz) of high explosive within a 6.35cm (2.5in) diameter metal sphere. A trained soldier can throw one to a distance of 40m (131ft), and its fragmentation pattern on explosion will kill within a 5m (16ft) radius and injure out to 15m (49ft).

Deploying any type of fragmentation grenade tends to follow a standard procedure. The grenade is clutched in the throwing hand with the fingers depressing the spring-loaded handle. The pin restraining this handle is then pulled with the non-throwing hand and the grenade is thrown at the target. As the grenade leaves the hand, the handle is released and a striker in the mechanism hits a percussion cap that, in turn, sets off a fuse with a time-delay burn of around four to five seconds. At the end of

Grenade practice involves building accuracy as well as distance. The thrower should also have available cover to protect her from her own grenade's explosion.

the time delay, the grenade explodes.

Tactically, hand grenades are an invaluable addition to the soldier's combat pack, particularly in urban combat and when clearing the enemy from bunkers or trench systems. (In close-quarters engagements, the soldier must be cautious about finding adequate cover to shield him from the effects of his own grenade detonation.) They also allow soldiers to engage an enemy who is out of line of sight. A useful tactical for grenade deployment is known as 'cooking off'. Here, the soldier pulls the grenade's pin and releases the handle prior to throwing – the soldier counts two full seconds before throwing the grenade. This technique has two main applications. The first is to prevent an enemy soldier having time to pick up the unexploded grenade and throw it back. The second is to give the grenade an airburst capability, exploding above the heads of an enemy in covered positions. Furthermore, cooking off is useful when throwing a grenade onto steeply inclined ground, as it ensures that the grenade will explode on the intended target and not roll away down the slope.

COMBAT DEMOLITIONS

The use of military-grade high explosives – which include materials such as TNT, RDX, C4, Semtex and PE.4 – tends to reside in the hands of combat engineers and specially trained demolitions experts. The definition of high explosive is a material that turns

into a large-volume gas instantly upon detonation, producing a massive blast effect. RDX explosive, for example, has a gas expansion velocity of 8350m/sec (27,400ft/sec). The applications of such destructive force are wider than might be expected. Within a combat context, demolitions are used for destroying bridges, buildings, vehicles, materiel and positions. They can also be used

A soldier prepares to throw a hand grenade from a trench. The pulling of the pin takes place at the same time as the 'cocking' of the throwing arm.

within anti-personnel booby traps, for cratering effects along enemy roads and runways, as well as in mine clearance. (The latter is particularly conducted with the Bangalore Torpedo, which consists of interlocking 1.5m/5ft

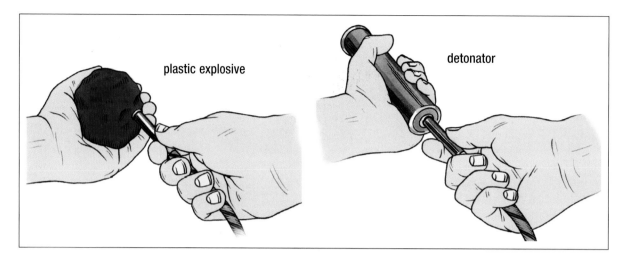

plastic explosive

detonator

long sections of tube, each containing 4.7kg/10.5lb of C4.) Non-combat applications include tree-cutting, altering watercourses and rapid earth clearance (useful for when ditches or trenches have to be dug at speed).

When faced with a demolitions task, the soldier must pick the type of explosive suited to that task. Modern military explosives come in several different configurations. Block demolition charges provide the explosives in a solid block, sometimes with an aperture in the end of the block for inserting the detonator. US Army TNT block demolitions, for example, come in 0.1kg (0.25), 0.22kg (0.5lb) and 0.45kg (1lb) blocks, and feature a threaded percussion cap well at one end.

Some of these block charges, the C4-filled M112 for example, can be cut to shape with a sharp blade to provide precise explosive control. Other block charges are actually made up of individual sheets: the M118 pack contains four flexible 0.22kg (0.5lb) C4

strips, each with its own adhesive backing to stick onto surfaces for cutting demolitions. Because of the flexibility of modern plastic explosives, explosives can even be wrapped around a spool, just like sticky tape.

The M186 roll demolition charge, for example, has 15m (50ft) of explosive wound around a plastic spool; the soldier simply cuts the explosive to the required length.

Block and strip explosives tend to be used for structure demolitions, cratering and engineering work. Multiple blocks can be combined into satchel charges for rapid, devastating use against enemy positions. Note also that blocks and packs of various types of explosive can be linked together by detonating cord to form a 'ring main', where all the explosives on the main detonate simultaneously. (Such is especially useful for building demolitions, where structures – particularly main support girders – need to be cut at the same

A detonator is the initiating device for an explosive. It can be simply pushed into a plastic explosive or engage with a dedicated detonator aperture in many other charges.

moment to achieve building collapse.)

A more specialist type of explosive is the shaped charge. Here, the explosive is embedded around a conical cavity lined with a material such as copper. When the charge is detonated, the lining is transformed into a high-velocity molten jet that cuts precisely through whatever structure it is directed towards. Shaped charges have dramatic penetrative properties, and so are useful against armoured vehicles and reinforced enemy structures. For example, a US 6.8kg (15lb) M2A4 shaped charge can punch through 76cm (30in) of reinforced concrete or 30cm (12in) of armour plate.

Using demolitions appropriately takes a lot of training and an advanced technical understanding of the explosives and structures that need to be demolished. A selection of typical tactical applications is given in the feature box 'Tactical demolitions'.

Taken together, the firepower of even a four-man fire team can have a formidable presence. Channelling that firepower into tactical manoeuvres, and balancing it with the many other tactical considerations on the battlefield, is governed by a broad series of Standard Operating Procedures (SOPs), which will be covered in our next chapter.

Members of a Navy and Marine Explosive Ordnance Disposal (EOD) take cover behind their Humvee as they destroy an improvised explosive device near Forward Operating Base Hit, Iraq.

TACTICAL DEMOLITIONS

ARTILLERY PIECES: The barrel of the artillery piece is blocked with earth or similar material to a depth of about 1m (3.3ft), just in front of the breech. A pack of appropriate explosive (such as C4) is then placed into the breech. The breech is closed just far enough to allow the detonating cord to snake out from the explosive charge. For self-propelled guns, other charges should be placed on the drive wheels. All charges are then detonated simultaneously.

ARMOURED FIGHTING VEHICLE (AFV): Place an 11kg (25lb) explosive charge within the hull of the AFV, or smaller charges on the driving, turret and gun controls. Stack the AFV's own ammunition around the charges and seal all hatches and slits. If explosives can only be placed externally, site them around the turret ring, engine compartment or wheel drive components, coordinated on a ring main.

BRIDGES: Place explosive packs on span junctions and supports. On supports, the packs should be sited on opposing sides at a slight offset angle to each other to increase the cutting effect. The aim is to make a minimum 5m (16ft) gap in the span to defeat enemy bridging technology.

CHAPTER TWO

INFANTRY TACTICS

To function coherently as part of an integrated military unit, every soldier must have a detailed, practical grasp of his army's Standard Operating Procedures (SOPs). The SOPs are the basic procedural guidelines for either undertaking a certain action or responding to a certain event. They are inculcated in training and reinforced in action, and experience has shown that the quality of SOP training will have a definite bearing on the soldier's survivability in action.

In this chapter we will examine the core skills of the modern professional soldier. Note that the emphasis here is on small-unit tactics – mainly fire team, squad and section levels. It is the skill and training at these levels that generally determines the outcomes of far larger defensive or offensive manoeuvres at the higher levels of organization.

September 2004: heavily armed US soldiers return to a CH47 Chinook helicopter after an operation in Afghanistan. Airborne deployment enables vertical envelopment of enemy positions, and rapid deployment to inaccessible areas.

ORGANIZATION AND PLANNING

The smallest element of most modern military units is the fire team. This consists of four soldiers, with a balanced mix of infantry firepower. In the US Army, the fire team is composed of a team leader of NCO (corporal/E-4 or sergeant/E-5) rank and three other infantrymen, one armed with an SAW to provide fire support and another (known as the grenadier) equipped with an M203 grenade launcher fitted to his M16 rifle. The fourth rifleman usually also handles the team communications.

The fire team structure offers several advantages. It promotes an intense bonding between its members, both in terms of unified responses and in psychological commitment to each member's welfare. In patrol

US Army soldiers conduct an area reconnaissance mission in Baghdad, Iraq. Note how each member of the patrol is taking responsibility for a different angle of observation.

situations, the four men each take a sector of observation, the sectors adding up to a 180-degree front or a 360-degree circular observation/fire response around the team. In attack or defence, a fire team will typically spread itself out over 50–100m (164–328ft), depending on circumstances, although larger distances can be covered if tactically appropriate or with the right communications.

Two fire teams are usually organized into a single squad (US Army) or section (British Army), and multiple sections form larger infantry formations, such as platoons. With each increase in size, the unit is capable of covering a greater frontage in attack or defence.

Planning infantry manoeuvres with these formations tends to

follow strict processes. In the US forces, the central method of mission planning is the METT-TC formula. The US Army Field Manual FM3-0, *Battle Command*, states that:

METT-TC refers to factors that are fundamental to assessing and visualizing: Mission, Enemy, Terrain and weather, Troops and support available, Time available, and Civil considerations.

Although the METT-TC formula tends to be thrashed out at command level, it is useful for and used in the tactical procedures of the small unit. Broken down, the considerations of METT-TC are as follows:

MISSION: The mission needs to be clearly defined, including final objective(s), the timeline of the operation and the purpose of the mission.

ENEMY: Enemy strengths and weaknesses need to be analyzed, including threats from both conventional and unconventional forces. 'Enemy' can be defined in its broadest sense to include factors such as the presence of disease in the operational area and problems affecting water/food supplies.

TERRAIN AND WEATHER: Information about terrain must be as complete as possible, including factors such as ground unsuitable for armoured vehicles, areas that could be prone to flooding, man-made or natural obstacles, the width of streets and bridges,

and the location of important objectives such as railroad terminals and airports. Weather data is especially important, as poor weather can turn solid ground into a quagmire and affect the possibilities of aerial resupply and close air support.

TROOPS AND SUPPORT AVAILABLE: This stage of the analysis matches the mission with the available troops. The commanders assess factors such as morale, units available, joint service support, civilian support and, critically, the logistical resources available to keep the mission or position sustainable.

TIME AVAILABLE: Here, the commanders assess every element of the mission timeline, from preparation and planning, through marshalling resources to the

actual timeframe for completing the mission.

CIVIL CONSIDERATIONS: The commanders should ensure that the mission has a minimal impact upon civilian economic and social life in the area. Soldiers need to be informed of local religious and social etiquette, and of the locations of potentially sensitive buildings, such as places of worship.

Once the METT-TC planning devolves down to the level of a section or fire team, the grand scale of the planning stage may well be lost. However, modern professional armies, particularly in the Western world, tend to provide even the humble private with a tactical and strategic overview. This gives individuals the ability to exercise purposeful

A squad of Royal Irish Rangers make use of an irrigation ditch to provide cover during a patrol in Afghanistan. The bank would provide protection from small arms and RPG fire.

initiative should their immediate commanders be injured.

PREPARATION FOR MOVEMENT

Movement in military terms refers to the techniques a soldier or unit uses to transfer from one position to another in a way that maintains maximum security and/or creates a manoeuvre advantage against the enemy. Movement actions include patrolling, attacking, deployment and withdrawing, and the unit that achieves superior movement usually dominates the battlefield. A major reason for the German *Blitzkrieg* victory in western Europe in 1940 was superior unit movements,

particularly by the Panzer divisions that used speed and directional ingenuity to throw less mobile British and French forces into disarray.

At a small-unit level, tactical movement is composed of the individual movement SOPs that every soldier should know, and the overall unit movement. These will be treated separately here, but the division is artificial, and in the field all personal movement would have to be integrated with unit tactical priorities.

The beginnings of any movement operation lie in preparation. A soldier's preparatory actions depend upon the mission, but the following are almost always essential:

● All weapons should be stripped and cleaned. Sights need to be zeroed (typically they are ranged out to 300m/984ft). Slings are adjusted for comfort.
● The appropriate inventory of kit is assembled. This will include ammunition, first aid supplies and specialist equipment (cutting gear, demolitions, etc). The kit is stowed appropriately in webbing and pack. In turn, any damage to load-carrying equipment should be repaired before movement commences.
● Personal camouflage is applied (see below).
● Health and hygiene preparation are vital. A soldier should have one or two days' worth of water and a similar duration of ration packs.

A patrol in Mogadishu in 1993 shows the typical composition of a squad or team, including a light machine gunner armed with an M249 and a rifleman with an M203 grenade launcher.

Any prophylactic medications should be taken, and changes of underwear must be carried to prevent sweat/wet-related injuries to groin or feet.
● All communications equipment is tested thoroughly, particularly within the context of the unit net. If the movement is likely to be a long one, spare batteries will be needed and these should also be tested.
● Most critically, the soldier should fully understand all orders, particularly his role in the

38

fulfilment of the mission brief and the roles that others in his unit will be playing.

BATTLEZONE MOVEMENT

When moving around a battlezone, a soldier's priority is to make maximum use of cover and concealment. Before moving from any position, the soldier should determine his next position based on a route offering the best available cover. This cover is anything that: a) prevents or limits the enemy's observation of the soldier's movement; and b) protects the soldier from enemy fire. Typical examples of good covered routes include trenches, depressions, riverbanks, urban features (such as walls, buildings, etc.), rubble or dense foliage. Before moving out from a covered position, the soldier should shift his position a few metres to the right or left, if possible – an

FIELD EQUIPMENT – USMC, VIETNAM, 1965

A US Marine private deployed to Vietnam in the mid-1960s would be heavily laden when setting out on patrol. A typical patrol kit would include two firearms, a 7.62mm (.3in) M14 or 5.56mm (.22in) M16 rifle and a .45 Colt M1911 handgun, with two spare magazines for the rifle and a spare clip for the pistol. Two or three fragmentation grenades were stored in pack pouches or from clips on webbing straps. The belt around the marine's waist would have a fighting knife, a first-aid kit and two canteens of water.

In the main pack were various items, including changes of socks and underwear, a poncho, three days' worth of rations, signal flares and smoke grenades. Other equipment carried in pouches or pockets included water purification tablets, anti-malaria pills and a map and compass. Taking into account a steel helmet, heavy flak jacket and the weight of the weapons, a marine could easily be carrying 36kg (80lb) of kit, a weight that made smooth tactical movement very difficult in the jungle terrain.

enemy soldier may have trained his weapon on the position where he saw the soldier take cover, and may be waiting for him to appear at the same spot to take his shot. Also, movement between covered

US troops training in a forest cover the ground ahead with an M60 machine gun and an M16 rifle. Their position is located so that the firepower is able to cover the main avenues of approach through the trees.

positions should take no more than three to five seconds; every second spent on the open gives the enemy greater opportunity for accurate weapon targeting. (The US Army remembers this point with the saying: 'I'm up – the enemy sees me – I'm down.')

However, when not in combat movement should be slow and steady, as sudden movements attract the eye more. As part of training, a soldier will have been instructed in several methods of physical movement: low crawl (on the belly), high crawl (on hands and knees) and rush. He should select the method appropriate to the terrain and situation, remembering that whatever he chooses, he must have enough time to move from cover to cover – he should never simply flop down in the open.

The soldier needs to be cautious about the type of cover he selects while under fire. Modern military ammunition is extremely powerful – a burst of 7.62mm (.3in) machine-gun fire, for example, will readily penetrate a single layer of brick or hack through an unarmoured vehicle's bodywork. If under fire, the best sort of cover is depressions in the earth, behind terrain landmarks such as hills, or behind major urban structures such as entire buildings. The cover should not be so restrictive, however, that the soldier is unable to deploy his own weapon conveniently.

AREAS TO AVOID

While moving around terrain, there are several areas the soldier should avoid. Naturally, open, flat areas are dangerous as they give the enemy clear fields of fire. The soldier should also avoid using cover that is too isolated – such as a solitary tree in the middle of the field – as he could find himself trapped there by enemy fire. The tops of hills and ridges are dangerous because the soldier can be silhouetted against the skyline. Steep or difficult terrain is avoided if possible, as it slows movement and often makes that movement noisy and conspicuous. Crossing open tracks or roads can also be a dangerous moment; a trained soldier will cross such obstacles at places that have the densest cover, sprinting rapidly across the road between covered positions.

A constant awareness of enemy movement is a priority. If the enemy cannot be seen,

A squad receiving artillery fire will aim to move out of the kill area as one unit, while maintaining plenty of space between each soldier to minimize the risk of casualties.

auditory signals can provide the best indication of his position, particularly gunfire. At night, the soldier should turn his head from side to side while cupping a hand behind his ear to improve directional awareness. Startled birds or other animals are other indications of an enemy presence. Where there are many civilians around, there can be some unusual enemy indicators. For example, in Iraq, normally vibrant streets may suddenly clear of women and children in the knowledge of attack. (In Northern Ireland, a whistle blast during a street riot sometimes caused the crowd to part, exposing a shooter firing from the back of a van that subsequently sped away.)

Conversely, the Iraq conflict has seen children ferrying ammunition across the streets prior to an ambush; the enemy knows that Allied rules of engagement forbid the targeting of children.

Face camouflage aims to break up the typical patterns of light and shade associated with the human face. It should be applied by a third party, as it is easy to miss areas on the face, even when using a mirror.

CCD PROCEDURES

In military terminology, CCD stands for Camouflage, Concealment, Decoy. It indicates the various strategies an infantryman has at his disposal for obscuring himself from the enemy or confusing the enemy as to his whereabouts. Camouflage refers to techniques of breaking up and merging a silhouette with the terrain. Simply moving amongst shadows, for example, degrades the outline clarity of a soldier's silhouette and makes him harder to see. In urban combat, this is why a soldier inside a building should stand back from the window inside the darkened room, even when firing his weapon, rather than lean out of the window and so present an easy 'framed' target.

UNIFORM

A soldier's most basic camouflage, however, is his uniform. The standard British 'Soldier 95' uniform, for example, is rendered in Disruptive Pattern Material (DPM), which has the usual woodland-type pattern of camouflage. Uniforms can be extremely effective camouflage, especially with the advent of the photo-realistic patterns that are emerging onto the civilian hunting market and are making their way through to some military units. The soldier needs to take care of his uniform. Many modern uniforms are printed with near-infrared reflectant dyes to provide some resistance to detection by night-vision devices, but too much starching will degrade these properties.

FOLIAGE

Foliage can also be applied to uniforms – mainly anchored to helmets and straps – to further break up the silhouette. Caution needs to be exercised here. Too much foliage can actually increase visibility by expanding the soldier's mass. Furthermore, the foliage camouflage will need

A soldier uses foliage added to a hat band to blend in to his surroundings. Note how he has correctly selected local foliage, and has used it to break up the shape of his head.

element that gives a soldier away. If a soldier moves too quickly, movement contrast with a static background reveals him. In a natural environment of irregular, soft lines, the straight metallic lines of a rifle stand out clearly. Applying foliage to a gun is not advisable, but camouflage paint can be applied to many parts to soften the straight lines. Alternatively, non-moving parts of the gun – particularly the barrel and stock – can be wrapped in pieces of camouflage material. Anything that shines should be darkened, and this particularly applies to bare skin. Camouflage paint is not applied to the whole face in a unitary colour – this would simply create a dark patch of contrast.

Instead, stripes of dark colour are pasted across those parts of the face that have most prominent shine characteristics – cheeks, nose, forehead, chin and ears. The shadow areas of the face, by contrast, receive light-coloured paint – around the eyes, under the chin and under the nose. The hands should be similarly covered, or gloves worn. If professional camouflage paints are not available, then burnt cork, charcoal, lampblack or mud can be used.

SOUND AND SMELLS

Camouflage is often identified only with the visual dimensions.

to be changed according to the environment; a soldier's brown-grass camouflage will be useless if he moves into a green-leaf woodland environment, and all foliage should be removed if he enters an urban environment. The rule is to select the camouflage material directly from the area of operation; that way the soldier ensures faithfulness with his surroundings. Note also that if leaves are used in camouflage, the soldier should present the top side of the leaves – typically the darker side – outwards, rather

than show the contrasting underside. All foliage, once cut, will degrade and brown over time, so it will need regular replacement if it is to stay convincing against a background of fresh growth, particularly in the summer months. Also, the broken ends of branches reveal the bright inner wood, something that stands out particularly well in moonlit conditions. These need to be camouflaged by smearing them with mud.

The important principle of these lessons is that *contrast* is the

However, sound and smells are just as important, especially at night. Before any operation, but particularly night actions, the soldier should tape down any parts of equipment that are prone to making noises. These include loose parts of a rifle (such as sling swivels), strap buckles and items such as canteens in packs. On certain rifles, wrapping tape around the safety catch can prevent a conspicuous click as the soldier prepares to open fire. The soldier tests for any equipment

When observing terrain, a soldier should divide it into set angles and distances, and then move his eyes methodically across every part of the scene, starting in the foreground.

NOISE SIGNATURES

Noise control is especially important at night, when even the slightest noises can travel over very long distances. The following give the distances over which the naked ear can detect common noise phenomena:

Noise Source	Distance detectable
Movement of troops on foot	
– Highway	up to 600m (1968ft)
– Dirt track	up to 300m (984ft)
Small arms weapon loading	up to 500m (1640ft)
Metal hitting metal	up to 300m (984ft)
Conversation of a few men	up to 300m (984ft)
Screams	up to 1500m (4921ft)
Motor vehicle on a highway	up to 1000m (3280ft)
Rifle shot	up to 3000m (9842ft)

(Information from US Army, FM 7-93, 'Long-Range Surveillance Unit Operations', 1995)

sounds by getting fully equipped and then jumping up and down on the spot. While on an operation, sounds can be kept to a minimum by using hand signals instead of verbal communications. In the British Army, for example, there are 40 different hand signals for section and platoon level operations, and every soldier should be familiar with them. These include:

HALT: Arm raised until hand is level with the shoulder. The number of fingers displayed on the hand indicates the duration of a rest in minutes.

ENEMY SPOTTED: Fist clenched with the extended thumb pointing downwards.

OBSTACLE: Arms crossed in front of the body.

RECONNAISSANCE: Hand circles the eye, like a child pretending to have a telescope.

ATTACK: A chopping action with the hand is made in the direction of the attack.

FORM AMBUSH: The hand first shields the eyes, then points in the direction of the ambush site.

Whoever is performing such hand actions, needs to make them easily understandable, but also make them as small as possible and without any jerky actions that will, in themselves, attract attention.

Another important element of noise discipline is choosing routes of manoeuvre that avoid noisy terrain surfaces, such as loose gravel or large amounts of dead leaves.

Olfactory discipline is, in many ways, more relevant to Special Forces personnel, who may well encounter enemy guard dogs during their operations. However, scent control is important to all soldiers, particularly in wilderness operations where artificial or human smells stand out among natural odours.

Human sweat gives out many of the odours present in the diet, so the soldier should avoid eating strongly scented foods – such as garlic and curries – before an operation. US soldiers in Vietnam reported that Viet Cong guerrillas hiding in close proximity were

Small open areas in woodland should never be crossed directly by a patrol. Instead it should use proximate cover to reach an agreed position.

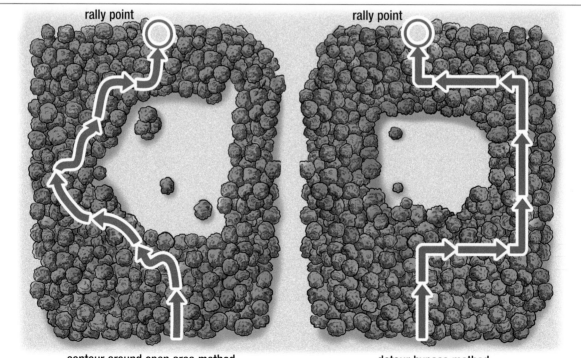

contour around open area method | detour bypass method

sometimes discovered by their scent, as their diet gave them a contrasting smell to the US troops. For similar reasons, strong soaps or aftershaves should also be avoided.

Naturally, smoking is an unacceptable risk on combat operations both in terms of the light source (a lighted cigarette at night is visible up to 0.8km/0.5 miles) and smell – cigarette smoke can be scented at up to 150m (492ft) away, given the right wind conditions.

DECOY

The final element of CCD is decoy. Decoy refers to anything that misleads the enemy. It includes making and emplacing dummy vehicles and positions (usually with the intention to fool enemy aerial reconnaissance), but also includes subterfuges such as air-dropping supply canisters to non-

existent forces, firing remotely controlled weapons from decoy positions and leaving fires burning at vacant positions.

In low-light conditions, a fire team manoeuvres through grassland. Gun muzzles must be kept off the floor at all times to avoid later malfunctions.

· DECOY ACTIONS

The greatest military deception operation in history was that put in place during the run-up to the D-Day invasion of Europe in 1944. Large areas of southern and eastern Britain were awash with wood-and-fabric dummy tanks and trucks, dummy landing craft and bogus radio traffic, resulting in the bulk of the German forces being deployed away from the Normandy beachheads on 6 June. Illustrating that such decoy techniques are not only relevant in less technologically sophisticated military periods, Serbian forces created thousands of decoy tanks during its

resistance against NATO in Kosovo in the late 1990s. These tanks were either wood-and-fabric constructions or inflatable types. Serbian AA guns had pushed NATO ground-attack aircraft to a bombing altitude of 4572m (15,000ft), high enough for the aerial observation platforms not to be able to tell the difference between real vehicles and dummy ones. For added authenticity, the Serbian fighters would put heaters under the dummies to create a thermal image for Allied night-vision devices. NATO forces wasted thousands of precision munitions destroying these dummies.

frontal cover

grenade sumps

Two types of trench – the top one is a simple slit trench with frontal cover, while the lower example is curved around the cover to enable the soldiers to fire directly to the front.

A well-prepared fighting position will have deep earth cover, fire-sector stakes to aid low-light shooting, and provide 360 degrees of observation between the members of the unit.

INFANTRY POSITIONS

When a soldier is not on manoeuvres, he is usually occupying some position or another. Sometimes this position is part of a manufactured complex – as is now seen in the vast US base in Baghdad – while on other occasions the soldier will have to create the fighting position from scratch.

In the latter case, there are distinct guidelines for improving the survivability of the position. As defined by the US Army, there are two simple criteria behind the creation of a fighting position. First, the soldier must be able to fight from the position, i.e. employ his weapon effectively. This means that machine-guns have full traverse, that riflemen have a good view over the surrounding terrain, and that grenades and possible support weapons such as mortars and anti-tank weapons can be deployed from the base and/or rim of the position. The second criterion relates to survivability. The US Army field manual FM 21-75, *Combat Skills of the Soldier*, states that: 'The cover of your fighting position must be strong enough to protect you from small arms fire, indirect fire fragments, and the blast wave of nuclear explosions.'

TRENCHES

At its simplest, a fighting position can consist of nothing more than a trench cut into the earth and big enough for one or two men. In a hasty combat situation, this trench can be nothing more than a carving in the earth about 46–50cm (18–20in) deep, just deep enough for the soldier to lie in. If time allows, however, a more substantial trench should be dug. It should be as deep as the soldier's armpits, allowing him to fire from the rim of the hole while keeping his torso protected. The hole should also be spacious enough so that the soldier can squat down inside it in the event of aerial bombing, artillery fire, etc, but small enough to minimize the effects of these threats, particularly when hiding from airburst munitions. Earth excavated during the digging of any trench fighting position is piled up in front and to the sides of the hole to provide additional cover, although a space of around 46cm (18in) is left between this earth and the rim of the hole to allow the soldier to prop his elbows on the parapet when firing. (Digging recesses in the parapet for the elbows also improves the accuracy of the rifle fire, or if the soldier is armed with a machine-gun, a recessed platform should be dug for the bipod legs.) Also, gaps should be left at the corners of the frontal cover, as these will allow the soldier to fire at an oblique angle out of the

position while remaining behind cover and also masking his muzzle flash.

Note that any position requires the same camouflage as soldiers. Any highly visible position is likely to be attacked directly, and is more likely to come in for the unwelcome attentions of enemy artillery and air attack. The most important point is to site the position in relation to already existing natural cover. A good location would be beneath trees and next to bushy outcrops – the foliage provides cover from both aerial and ground

observation. (Surrounding ground cover, however, should not be so thick that it allows an enemy to make a flanking approach unobserved.) The surplus earth stacked around the hole should be masked with local foliage. If naturally occurring overhead cover does not exist, some can be manufactured using boards and supports covered with either

Trench digging is an exhausting skill, but to maximize his survivability a soldier should be able to create a basic but deep hole within an hour. The ideal depth is armpit height.

camouflage net or foliage, preferably both. Note that the floor of the fighting position should also be littered with local vegetation to shield the bare earth from aerial photography.

Another valuable addition to a fighting position is to cut grenade sumps into the floor. These are narrow, straight holes that go down into the hole for a depth of 0.75–1.5m (2–5ft). If the enemy throws a grenade into the hole, the defender simply kicks it into one of the sumps. Although the subsequent detonation will still be dangerous, the ground will soak up much of the fragmentation effect and blast.

In densely wooded terrain the nature of a fighting position changes. Tree roots running through the soil can make digging impossible. Sometimes a fighting position can be partially dug into the base of an earthen bank or even around a large tree stump. Several cut tree trunks can be used as frontal, rear and flanking cover – whatever is used, surrounding protection should be at least 46cm (18in) thick. Soldiers must check the condition of trees carefully before locating a fighting position under them – high winds can bring down lethally heavy deadwood branches. Another important environmental consideration is the presence of water. Nearby rivers and streams can break their banks in heavy downpours and flood a fighting position. Rain itself can flood a position if the position is placed in basins in the land, so slightly elevated positions are recommended.

TRENCH VARIATIONS

Beyond simple trenches, a wide range of fighting positions are available for multiple people. For example, trenches can be cut in a U-shape, bent around a large piece of frontal cover such as a rocky outcrop, or two trenches can be cut side by side in a V pattern with earth piled up between them. A T-shaped trench offers the vertical line of the T for ammunition storage, or to provide a position for rear protection. The important point of any fighting position is that it must be designed for combat. Sectors of fire are a major consideration. In the case of multiple positions, the fire sectors of one should interlock with the near fire sector of the next. This creates interlocking fire without any fire gaps. Within a single position, two or more

Trench clearance requires a rapid and constant tempo and a violent use of small arms. Grenades should precede any movement around a corner or into a bunker, and teams should split up to cover all avenues along the trench simultaneously.

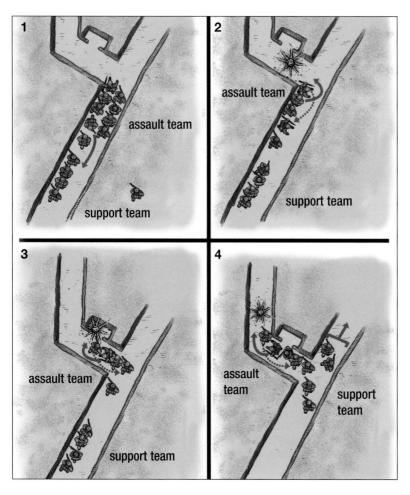

BUNKER COMBAT

The United States discovered to its cost the advantages of well-camouflaged bunkers during its island-hopping campaign in the Pacific in 1943–45. Japanese coastal bunkers on Iwo Jima were constructed from a mix of palm trunks, sand and concrete, and were so well camouflaged that often the only signs of their presence were gun flashes from the firing slits. Similarly, the Japanese on Okinawa utilized caves and rock outcrops in the interior of the island to create almost undetectable bunker complexes; these were frequently enhanced with concrete structures and lavishly covered with local foliage. Often, only intensive US flamethrower fire revealed hidden bunkers by stripping them of foliage cover. Interestingly, in the conflict between Israel and the Hezbollah groups of Lebanon (ongoing at the time of writing), Israeli Defence Forces (IDF) units have noticed that Hezbollah fighters have utilized similar camouflage tactics, creating vegetation-covered positions to obscure heavy weapons and ambush units in the rocky terrain of southern Lebanon. Furthermore, individual Hezbollah fighters have been attempting to move around the landscape entirely disguised as trees or bushes. Although such tactics have been partially successful, Israeli weaponry – as with the US in the Pacific – has inflicted a heavy toll on the guerrillas while being used in a 'reconnaissance by fire' mode.

soldiers must designate their respective fire sectors if they are not to duplicate fire and waste ammunition. Each soldier positions two sector stakes – pieces of wood or other material about 46cm (18in) long – in front of his immediate position in the trench. The gap between these two stakes marks out his field of fire. In a two-man trench, the sector stakes are usually positioned so that each soldier is firing out to the oblique angles of the trench, away from each other but interlocking with adjacent positions.

Aiming stakes are another useful addition. These are short stakes – preferably forked branches – driven into the ground that act as aiming guidance indicators for the rifleman. He lines them up with dangerous areas – such as known enemy positions or potential lines of approach – and can use them during low-light or night-time conditions to be able to switch his fire around accurately.

A good fighting position provides excellent security to professional forces, although it

A grenade sump in action – the sloping platform running along the base of the trench channels the grenade down into a hole. The earth will then absorb most of the grenade blast.

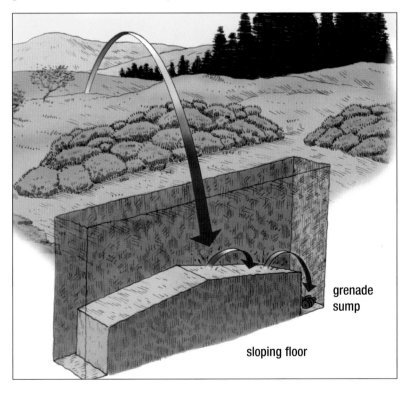

grenade sump

sloping floor

should be noted that developments in modern weaponry are threatening to render the trench obsolete. Modern handheld grenade launchers, for example, can fire airburst munitions that will – having been fed with precise range information from laser equipment – explode directly above a trench with lethal downward fragmentation effects. Airburst technologies from artillery and air power have also married up with global positioning satellite (GPS) precision. In short, if the position is detected, its survivability is precarious, particularly if you are not a soldier of a modern, professional army.

UNIT MOVEMENT – PLANNING

Successful unit movement requires both rigorous coordination between all the unit members, combined with intelligent initiative on the part of each soldier. While there are clear training guidelines for successful unit movement – including factors such as spacing between soldiers, procedures for setting up ambushes and attack formations – these are guidelines only, and will be flexibly applied on the battlefield. Here, we will focus on unit manoeuvres up to squad level.

Regardless of the objective, all unit manoeuvres have certain fundamentals. US Army Ranger training provides the following guidelines for successful squad/ platoon movements. They should be clearly controlled by the leader, ideally with arm-and-hand signals, only resorting to radio contact when absolutely necessary. During both movement and halts, the unit has to maintain 360-degree security, with only a 25 per cent reduction in alert status during the halts. Each individual must have a clearly defined responsibility, as well as a definite purpose in fulfilling the METT-TC criteria. Fire support options should be coordinated before the operation commences. This includes notifying available support assets (artillery, air force units etc) of the unit's objective and proposed route of travel. Using intelligence and mapwork, the leader can pre-plan fire support at key locations along the route of travel, if appropriate. The *Ranger Handbook* further explains the role of support fire in movement operations:

US troops in Afghanistan. Mountain ops present severe environmental challenges, and these must in turn be accounted for in the tactical planning as much as enemy activity.

Having a fire plan gives you a tool to help you move or navigate. For example, you can aid detection by planning fires at known points along the route: you can avoid detection by planning fires to destroy known enemy sensor fields or observation posts; you can have fires planned to divert the enemy's attention away from an area through which the patrol is moving; you have fire planned and ready to engage any threat to the patrol.

(US Army, *Ranger Handbook*, 1992)

Good route planning is vital for a successful unit manoeuvre. Depending on a mission, the considerations can be almost unlimited in number, but the unit leaders should take into account the following considerations:

● To avoid enemy detection, the unit's route of travel should incorporate the best available cover and concealment. The route should also be planned in stages (known in British terminology as 'legs'), moving between observation and halt positions, where the mission progress is reviewed.
● Alternative routes of movement – both outward and return journeys – should be planned as options for responding to unexpected developments.
● The route must constantly take into account possible or known enemy positions. If the purpose of the operation is to avoid the enemy, high-risk manoeuvres are best confined to the early stages of the operation, as it increases the

This series of diagrams shows some of the basic principles of concealment for travel manoeuvres. Each case shows the best routes for staying out of sight and for finding cover should the patrol suddenly come under fire.

chances of the entire manoeuvre going undetected.

● Good fire positions and fire should be noted along the route of travel, in case they are required in an emergency later.

Of course, it is one matter to plan a route precisely, but quite another to follow that route, particularly through difficult terrain. Observation and navigation skills are therefore critical.

UNIT OBSERVATION AND NAVIGATION

Before moving over any piece of ground, the soldier needs to scan that ground to note its features and signs of enemy presence. This must be a methodical action that requires mental and visual discipline. A sound method is to divide, mentally, the ground into three horizontal sections – foreground, middle ground and distance – with one central division running straight out from the soldier. This division creates six portions of ground. Each portion is scanned in turn, the soldier moving his eyes systematically from right to left, and top to bottom, of each segment. As he scans, he looks for anything unusual or important, such as a camouflage position or an enemy vehicle, and then reports this to his unit commander (see below for target identification procedures).

DISTANCE JUDGEMENT

Good military observation skills also rely heavily on distance judgment. If the soldier cannot accurately estimate distance, he will under- or overestimate the length of time it will take to cover ground, and also have poor fire control. The easiest method of distance judgment is the unit of measure. Here, the soldier familiarizes himself with a standard unit of measure – such as a 100m (328ft) shooting range or a fixed-length sports track – then mentally applies this to the terrain in front of him. Note that the unit of measure method is typically accurate only to distances of around 400m (1312ft), and has diminished accuracy

Paratroopers from the 82nd Airborne Division conduct a presence patrol in the flooded French Quarters district of New Orleans. The patrol members observe proper combat spacing.

A patrol should have primary and secondary routes of deployment (represented by the large and small arrows respectively) to give it a flexible response to events.

if sections of the ground between the soldier and target cannot be seen.

If the soldier finds it awkward to judge the distance of a far object, then he can use a technique known as bracketing. Here, the overall distance is mentally bisected, or even divided into quarters if necessary. The soldier then uses the unit of measure method to estimate the quarter or half distance, and multiplies the result appropriately to give the final distance. To aid his distance judgment, the soldier can also train himself to identify size differences of familiar objects – people, vehicles, buildings, etc – at set distances, and apply these to distance judgments in the field. One point to note is that the apparent distances to objects change according to environmental conditions. On bright days, for example, objects can seem closer, although sunlight in the eyes or poor lighting conditions can also make objects appear smaller. Distance judgment is made more complex when looking across valleys or other empty spaces, or when looking along roads or tracks at ground level – both situations reduce the amount of visual references used to make the distance judgement.

Distance judgment must also be made while on the move, as well as from static positions. To calculate distance travelled, the soldier uses a 'pacing scale'. This is based on the number of paces it takes for the soldier to cover 100m (328ft). Pacing scales vary according to the type of terrain – smaller steps are taken in jungle terrain, for example, than along an open road. The soldier will formulate a series of pacing scales by, under non-operational conditions, pacing out 100m (328ft) in various terrain conditions. When the soldier is on an operation, counting paces will aid navigation and inform the unit of how much progress is being made.

FLASH-TO-BANG
Another technique for calculating the distance to weapon target is the flash-to-bang technique. This is based on a calculation using the speed of sound, which is 350m/sec (1148ft/sec). If, therefore, one second elapses between the soldier seeing the flash of a weapon and hearing the bang,

that weapon is 350m (1148ft) away and so on. The flash-to-bang technique is not the most accurate method of distance judgment, but can be used quickly in a combat situation. Of course, there are many different technological aids to distance judgment. Consulting an accurate map is one of the best guides to distance, and laser range finders, GPS systems and aerial observation information provide the highest-quality distance and location information.

DESCRIBING TARGET LOCATIONS
Observation also concerns accurately describing target locations to other members of the unit. A basic method for doing this, as taught by the British Army, involves simple divisions of an imaginary 180-degree arc extending out from the soldier across the terrain in front of him. With the soldier positioned at the bottom centre of the arc, the line of view straight ahead is known as the axis of arc. The lines

1st, 2nd & 3rd squads
MG = machine-gun crew
MW = medium weapons

extending straight out either side of the soldier are simply known as left and right. The angles from the axis of arc to left or right are subdivided into quarter, half and three-quarters. When identifying a target, the soldier will give the distance, the angle of location and a description of the target. For example: '200 – quarter left – parked vehicle.' If the target is slightly at variance with the quarter angle, it can be modified: '200 – quarter left – slightly right – parked vehicle.'

CLOCK METHOD

Sometimes more precision is required in identifying a target, and here the soldier can use the clock method. First, he identifies a conspicuous point using the method above. However, once that point is identified, it then becomes the centre of an imaginary clock face, with the 12 placed directly in line with the angle of identification. Using the clock, the soldier can then specify a target more accurately. For example: '250 – half right – radio antenna – 7 o'clock – concealed gun.' (Note that the dashes here indicate pauses. Any command should have pauses between the elements, to give listeners a space of time in which to absorb each piece of information.)

Alongside the techniques of observation outlined above, all soldiers in a unit must have sound navigational skills. Space does not allow us to study the actual techniques of orientation, but within a unit context, several people should be designated as navigators, and several others as pacers. Navigators should be

Using the points of an imaginary clock is a quick way for units to communicate target positions. Note the interlocking fields of MG fire here.

trained fully in compass orientation, as well as in the use of GPS navigation tools.

UNIT FORMATIONS AND MOVEMENT

Although there are some slight doctrinal differences between armies, the principles of unit formations and movement are generally universal. In terms of formations, for example, British Army doctrine advocates five different section (two fire teams) structures. The type of formation selected depends on many different factors, including enemy fire, terrain and required speed of movement.

Also note that in any formation the individual soldiers should be spread out, with a minimum of 10m (32ft) between each man. This prevents single artillery shells from wiping out an entire section, or from an enemy machine-gunner easily acquiring a group target. However, the spacing between the members of the unit should not be even; irregular spacing makes enemy target acquisition even more difficult.

SINGLE FILE: Here, the whole section is strung out in a single column. This pattern is often dictated by terrain – such as moving along a jungle trail – but has the advantages of speed and ease of control, especially at night. Each soldier should alternate his direction of observation (one looks right, one looks left and so on) to cover all angles. Major disadvantages of the formation are its vulnerability to oblique or enfilade fire, particularly from a heavy machine-gun, and the difficulty in deploying heavy frontal firepower when needed.

FILE: The section splits up the fire teams. Each fire team then marches in single file but parallel to one another. The file formation has many of the advantages and disadvantages of single file, but gives the unit strong flank responses to enemy attack.

DIAMOND: The diamond formation is constructed in the shape of its name, and is primarily for use by the section when it is travelling through open terrain at night.

It provides a 360-degree surveillance coverage around the unit, with each person having an allocated observation sector. As such, the diamond can respond to frontal, rear and flanking attacks The section commander can be placed either at the front of the diamond, or in its middle to aid quieter communication.

ARROWHEAD: The arrowhead is another open-ground formation. It is shaped like a triangle, with one soldier in the centre of the flat base and the others distributed equally up to the point. The arrowhead is very good for responding to frontal attacks, as it can generate large amounts of firepower in that direction. Against flanking attacks, it is more difficult to control.

EXTENDED LINE: This formation is a lateral version of single file – all the soldiers are positioned side by side in a space line. Extended lines are usually used in fast attacking manoeuvres, when all soldiers need to arrive at their destination at the same time. Furthermore, the diamond and arrowhead formations described above may move into extended line, should they come under frontal attack.

While the formations give each fire team member a specific role, there are other relations between units, up to company level, that are used for tactical

PATROL PLANNING

The planning phases of a patrol are essential for operational success. Critical considerations include:

● Light and weather conditions – these can have a major impact upon the patrol timetable.
● Specialist personnel needed (dog handlers, snipers, engineers, etc).
● Organization of fire support. Artillery and air support controllers need to be informed of the precise routes taken by the patrol, and need to agree on safe fire coordinates and possible targets.
● Establishing communications protocols within the patrol and headquarters and support elements.
● Fixing passwords to allow safe return to friendly lines.

● Routes to and from the objective, divided into primary and alternate routes. The alternate routes are for use in case the primary routes become compromised by enemy activity.
● Setting unit formations for the patrol, including the appropriate composition of firepower for the mission and the location of team or squad leaders.
● Setting objective rally points (ORPs) along the patrol route. These act as places for rest, intelligence sharing or as fallback positions in case the patrol comes under heavy engagement.
● Contingency drills – these are response procedures to cover a multitude of different outcomes, including handling unexpected enemy prisoners or separation of patrol units.

A section of US Marines engage enemy forces with their M16A2 rifles on the outskirts of Baghdad during the opening phase of the invasion of Iraq, April 2003.

movements. In the US Army, three types of movement are advocated: Travelling, Travelling Overwatch and Bounding Overwatch. These are used to control the distances between individual soldiers and/or distances between individual units. Here, we will look at these three formations in the context of a US squad, but they can be scaled up to major operations (simply replace fire teams with squads, platoons, companies, etc). Note that the following are systems of movement, not manoeuvre. Manoeuvre refers to the tactical movements during actual combat

– some of these will be studied below – whereas movement means the techniques of moving units through a battlespace while being prepared to meet action (although they also have applications while in combat).

TRAVELLING FORMATION

In simple Travelling formation, there is 10m (32ft) distance between each individual and 20m (64ft) space between squads. The squads are positioned in line with each other, with the squad leader the rearmost member of the first fire team. Travelling formations allow one squad to move up in support of another if it is attacked, and also provide good flanking security.

For good firepower control, the front fire team places its SAW gunner on the right or left flank,

while the rear fire team has its gunner on the opposite flank. Travelling movement is used when maximum speed needs to be attained and the chances of meeting enemy forces are minimal.

TRAVELLING OVERWATCH

The Travelling Overwatch formation is an extension of Travelling, but is used when there is an increased likelihood of enemy contact. Here, the rear fire team is at least 50m (164ft) behind the front fire team, and is designated as the 'overwatch' element. This element 'watches over' the front unit, maintaining visual and communication contact, and will use the increased space to provide better manoeuvre options should the frontal element come under attack. The keyword in this movement is flexibility – the relationship between the two elements should alter depending upon the terrain and circumstances.

BOUNDING OVERWATCH

The Bounding Overwatch movement is used when there is a strong likelihood of enemy contact. Here, the two units maintain a similar distance apart as in Travelling Overwatch. However, while one unit stays in a static security position as the overwatch element, the other 'bounding' element moves from behind into positions ahead of the overwatch element. Then the two units swap roles.

Bounding Overwatch provides maximum security, as the bounding element moves under the dedicated cover of the overwatch element. Note that the Bounding Overwatch is subject to many variations, but the basic principle of 'one moving, one covering' stands.

FIRE CONTROL

The Bounding Overwatch can also be transferred into a combat tactic, otherwise known as 'fire-and-manoeuvre'. Here, a unit advances towards or retreats from an enemy in steps. One unit, say a fire team, is static and pours covering fire onto the enemy position to suppress incoming fire. While they cover, the other fire team moves up (in the case of an advance), then drops down to take over the covering fire role as the other fire team moves up and through.

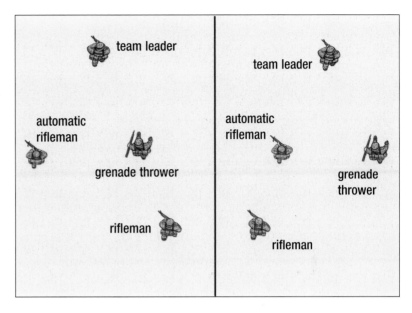

The fire team wedge is a useful squad formation that provides an excellent basis for responding to frontal attack. The two examples here show how the firepower can be distributed differently between the members of the formation.

UNIT MANOEUVRE

A near-textbook, real-life example of a unit manoeuvre in combat conditions is that famously undertaken by Easy Company, 2nd Battalion, 506th Parachute Infantry Regiment, 101st Airborne on 6 June 1944.

Easy Company, under the acting command of Lieutenant Richard Winters, was given the task of destroying a battery of German 105mm howitzers firing at the Allied landings on Utah Beach. With a group of 13 men, Winters reconnoitred and discovered the battery just south of the village of Le Grand-Chemin. The German position consisted of four 105mm (4.13in) guns and several MG42 machine-gun nests, all connected by a hedgerow-lined trench network and manned by around 50 men. Despite the numerical disadvantage, Winters led his unit into the attack. Two M1919 .30 calibre machine-guns established the base of fire, which was enhanced by another group of soldiers providing flanking fire. Under this cover, Winters then led an assault team down the enemy trenchline, systematically clearing the gun positions. The assault relied heavily on grenades, which were thrown into the gun positions or around the angles of the trench to clear the way for small-arms assault. The final gun position was cleared by reinforcements from Dog Company commanded by Lieutenant Ronald Spiers. The final casualties for this raid were four dead and two wounded on the US side, but 15 dead and 12 prisoners on the German side, with many more wounded.

The result is that the squad 'leapfrogs' toward the enemy in stages, but at no point loses its covering fire.

More will be said about attack manoeuvres later on, but here we will look at fire control, the essential ingredient of any combat success. The first element of fire control is command. The team or squad leader will need to give clear fire orders to his unit. He does this using a formula similar to that described above for target designating, which is known as the GRIT formula:

G – Group: the leader says which group the fire command is intended for.
R – Range: the leader states the range to the target in metres.
I – Indication: he explains where to look.
T – Type: defines the type of fire that is needed.

In terms of type of fire, the leader has several options, both in terms of volume of fire and timing. The leader can order immediate burst or rapid fire at the objective, meaning the unit should open up with everything it has until either the target is neutralized or the leader calls a halt. Trained soldiers should, however, keep an eye on ammunition conservation.

When first contact is made, the rule is to generate immediate heavy fire but slacken the pace of fire after a few seconds to stop guns overheating and to save ammunition. The leader can also designate a time for firing to commence. This could be a specific time, such as 0600 hours, or an opportunistic moment, such as 'fire when enemy soldiers appear'. A full GRIT order, therefore, could look like the following: 'No.2 Squad – 250 – half left, enemy trench – rapid fire when enemy appears.'

PATROL OPERATIONS

Patrolling is one of the most common unit missions. Patrols can have several, often overlapping, purposes. There are reconnaissance patrols, where a unit conducts a systematic in-depth reconnaissance of a particular terrain zone. Tracking patrols purposely attempt to locate an enemy force, while combat patrols – which is what tracking patrols often turn

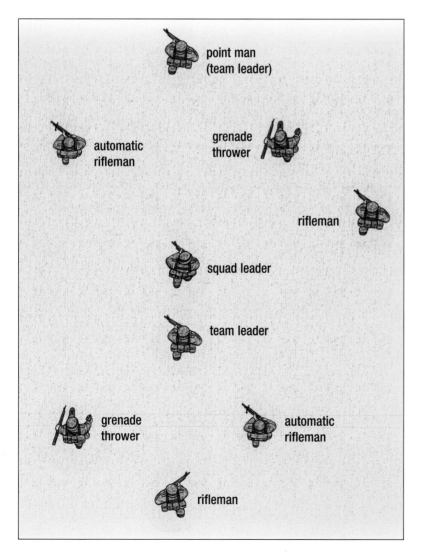

point man
(team leader)

automatic
rifleman

grenade
thrower

rifleman

squad leader

team leader

grenade
thrower

automatic
rifleman

rifleman

A patrol must combine movement, protection and observation. This formation has good front and rear strength, with the squad leader probably in the top middle position.

into – are for the destruction of equipment, positions or personnel, or to provide cover for other patrols or manoeuvres.

All patrols have very intensive planning phases, using all available intelligence. The patrol commander will first examine all available paper and photographic intelligence and also, if possible, recce the intended patrol route from observation posts (OPs). Patrol planning will include a full METT-TC analysis, with particular focus upon the routes of outward and return travel and the setting of rally points (ORPs) along the way.

Once the plan has been formulated, the patrol leader will then brief all patrol members. In the British Army, the briefing –

which is usually conducted with the aid of mapwork or a sandtable – takes the following format:

1. Ground – physical description of patrol terrain.
2. Situation – status of enemy and friendly forces in the patrol area.
3. Mission – clear explanation of the patrol mission.
4. Execution – the primary and alternate routes to objective, the action at the objective, timing and coordination, security measures, fire plan, etc.
5. Service support – the physical practicalities of the patrol, such as ammunition allocation, specialist equipment and medical supplies.
6. Command and signal – the communications procedures throughout the patrol.

Fire teams should operate in mutually supporting manoeuvres. Here the team at the top left provides cover as another team crosses the brow of a hill. A rear unit acts as security and a reserve.

In terms of execution, a patrol may follow one of several tactical route methods for moving between the start point and the final objective. At its simplest, the patrol may move in along a single line between A and B, returning by a different line of travel. Such a patrol is known as a route reconnaissance, and is usually used for patrolling a certain feature, such as a road or river. It has limited reconnaissance value, however.

A Fan Patrol covers much more ground. Here, the patrol

stops at regular objective rally points (ORPs) along the route of travel. From here patrol teams make further individual patrols, following a roughly circuitous route from and to the ORP. Taken together, the mini patrols cover all of the terrain around the ORP, and when diagrammatically represented give the appearance of 'fan blades' spreading out from the centre.

A different method of maximizing patrol ground coverage is the Converging Routes method. Here, the patrol consists of multiple teams, all of whom take different but converging routes through to a final ORP. A variant on this is the Successive Sectors method, whereby the

US soldiers provide security while their team members prepare to pull out a Stryker vehicle that is stuck in the mud during a patrol in Mosul, Iraq, June 2006.

patrol meets at all the individual ORPs, but uses a Converging Routes strategy between each of those positions. There are many other permutations of patrol routes, and much will depend upon the specific context (particularly terrain and enemy) of the mission.

Patrols are vulnerable to many factors, not least a continual exposure to the elements and the possibility of enemy ambush. Therefore, the following measures are put in place to improve patrol survivability and efficiency:

SECURITY: CCD measures must be in place throughout the patrol, particularly at ORPs (see below). Radio communications are kept to a minimum. During any stop, no matter how temporary, security elements should fan out around the patrol. If a position is to be occupied for more than a few hours, fighting positions should be established.

ORP PROCEDURE: During long patrols, ORP discipline can make the difference between a successful or failed patrol. The following procedures must take place. All personnel are checked off as present.

Fire positions and/or shelters are established if necessary. Essential equipment (communications, surveillance devices, etc) is checked and weapons are cleaned. Ammunition supply is checked and, if necessary, magazines refilled.

Personal hygiene – soldiers will wash and change socks and underwear, and the patrol medic may conduct skin inspections. A latrine is dug at a respectable distance from the ORP. Sentries and other security teams are posted. The next phase of the operation is clarified and discussed. When leaving the ORP, all signs of presence are removed to deny the enemy intelligence.

Good communication is central to effective troop operations. The leader should speak in clear, simple sentences, with pauses between each so that the information is absorbed.

INTELLIGENCE CONSOLIDATION: The intelligence gathered by all members of the patrol must be coherently collected. Information should be passed to team leaders and up to the patrol leader or intelligence officer. The patrol will have to undergo a thorough debriefing on return, so this information collection is vital.

RETURN TO LINES PROCEDURE: Returning to friendly lines is actually a dangerous moment for the patrol, as they might be mistaken for the enemy. All parties should be familiar with passwords and the timetable for return (with contingency procedures) should be in the hands of all relevant personnel, particularly sentries.

COMBAT PATROL: AMBUSHES

The classic outcome of a combat patrol is an ambush. Note that the enemy can initiate the ambush instead of the patrol, particularly if the patrol's security has been compromised at some point. Here, we will look at the tactics for both implementing ambushes and responding to ambush attacks.

The primary purpose of an ambush is to destroy enemy troops and materiel via a surprise concentration of heavy firepower. In doing so, the ambush party not only inflicts attrition on the

enemy, it also creates a wider impact by affecting the area security of enemy movements, logistics and bases. Ambushes are either pre-planned – the best type – or are improvised at speed on the basis of unexpected enemy contact.

Location is the most important factor in setting up an ambush. The USMC document 'Conduct of the Patrol 2', issued as part of the Basic Officer Course, describes

the qualities of 'favourable terrain' for an ambush:

Select an area for ambush in which the enemy is canalized between two natural or existing obstacles whereby his opportunity to attack or escape is limited. The ambush patrol should have maximum cover and concealment, not only for firing positions, but also for routes of withdrawal. The enemy should be offered as little protection from fire as possible.

A combined British and Iraqi National Guard patrol moves along in a column during a patrol in Al Amarah, Iraq. Columns are the best formations for very fast movement, and are suited to roads or other narrow terrain.

AMBUSH

The ideal terrain for an ambush is where the ambush party is set back in heavy cover – such as the edge of a wood or behind rocky outcrops – while the enemy is either strung out along a narrow and exposed route, or fixed within a base or position.

A deliberate ambush requires much planning. The ambush party is split into two or three groups, depending on numbers. One group is the ambush group – the unit that will actually launch the ambush. Either side of the ambush group are flanking units, known in the British Army as stop groups. These provide warning of the enemy's approach, but also serve to cut off or harass the

enemy after the ambush is sprung. If numbers allow, a security group is established behind the ambush group. All elements will have a common ORP, usually positioned behind the security group, to which they will move once the ambush is completed.

The area in which the enemy will be attacked is known as the kill zone. If time is available, the ambush group may prepare the kill zone with obstacles, booby traps, mines or trip flares. It then positions its heavy firepower along the kill zone, with machine-guns and AT weapons often concentrated at either ends – this traps the enemy column or unit between the heaviest fire, while also allowing lethal oblique and

interlocking fire patterns. When the enemy is approaching the kill zone, the flanking units give a silent warning. The ambush group commander will allow as many of the enemy to enter the kill zone as possible before giving a prearranged signal to open fire. The signal itself must produce casualties, such as a burst of machine-gun fire, because a non-lethal signal will give the enemy a tiny window in which to flinch and take cover. The ambush group, with a minimum of 5m (16.4ft) between each man, will then pour maximum full-auto firepower onto the enemy, concentrating on groups of soldiers, enemy soldiers manning heavy firepower vehicles (such as machine-guns or rocket launchers) and significant materiel – anything to maximize destruction within the window of the ambush.

Vehicles at the front and rear of a column should be disabled first to trap other vehicles in between, and the ambush group should try to prevent troops disembarking from trucks (this is done by one soldier shooting the body of the truck, while another shoots up the tailgate area). If the enemy is crumbling, the ambush group should close up to them to prevent the enemy finding cover or organizing a defence. An auditory or visual signal brings the ambush to a close based on an agreed outcome (the enemy is destroyed or in retreat), or if the ambush has failed.

The ambush may have several outcomes. If the enemy is totally

TALIBAN AMBUSH

The Taliban insurgents of Afghanistan have long used ambush as their primary insurgency tactic. During the Soviet occupation of Afghanistan between 1979 and 1989, Soviet vehicular columns were particularly vulnerable in Afghanistan's winding terrain. Mujahideen fighters would lever a boulder or fell a tree onto a narrow mountain road to stop a convoy, and then wait until vehicle occupants had disembarked before opening fire. Similar tactics are now being used in Afghanistan's troubled Helmand province, where British, US and Afghan forces are struggling against a rising insurgency. For example, on 10–11 October 2005, an Afghan police convoy slowed to cross a mountain river. However, up to 60 Taliban guerrillas had positioned themselves behind surrounding rocks to create devastating interlocking fields of fire. Their firepower was purely small arms, a mix of AK rifles and Soviet-era machine-guns. When the ambush was sprung, however, 19 of the Afghan police were killed and five went missing, probably taken as captives by the Taliban. Four police vehicles were completely destroyed by the intensity of the fire.

The RPG-7 (left) and the AK assault rifle are the principal tools fuelling many of the world's insurgencies. In Iraq and Afghanistan, the RPG-7 is one of the main ambush weapons, fired at close-range from urban cover.

destroyed or subjugated, an assault group may then enter the kill zone to obtain intelligence or prisoners. Alternatively, if the enemy is mounting a successful counter-ambush defence, or nearby enemy reinforcements are expected, all elements will withdraw to the ORP for consolidation then escape from the ambush zone.

RESPONDING TO AMBUSH

We will now look at ambushes from the other side. For a unit that is the victim of a sudden ambush, the correct response is critical. This response is not simply to try to escape the kill zone – a well-planned ambush will have covered all

For a long target, such as an enemy column, multiple ambush points are best to cause maximum disruption. These have to be effectively coordinated by radio.

the escape routes. Instead the unit should respond by *immediately* returning as much firepower as possible at the enemy. In this way it may actually pin the ambush group in place, allowing sub-units to break out and try to attack the enemy from the flanks.

Advancing straight at the enemy can also weaken its fire as it has to readjust its positions under the threat, but ideally the unit should move to attack the ambusher's flanks. If distance from the enemy allows, the unit should also call in artillery and air support, although the proximity of the ambush may disallow this.

Prevention of an ambush is naturally a much better policy than attempting to survive an ambush. Studies in Vietnam showed that ambush prevention or survival was greatly improved through the following measures:

1. Disperse a unit through the terrain either side of a main route of travel. That way, the unit encounters the enemy on its flank and keeps the bulk of its troops out of the kill zone.
2. All units, including vehicular convoys, should have flank and rear security, while advance scouts reconnoitre the ground ahead.
3. In the case of vehicular convoys, heavily armed escorts should be distributed along the length of the convoys. Vehicles should be spaced enough to allow easy emergency manoeuvres, but be close enough to provide rapid support to each other if necessary.
4. Units can improve survivability by having quick reaction groups purposely trained in ambush response.

These measures made a significant impact on the success rates of NVA/Viet Cong ambushes,

and are still implemented in Iraq, Afghanistan and other world war zones.

ATTACKING MANOEUVRES

Attacking manoeuvres come in an almost infinite range. Every military objective is unique, as are the human and material resources available to the attacking units. Doctrinal examples of offensive and defensive manoeuvres are known as battle drills, and we shall look at some key examples here.

In general theory, attacks (certainly up to platoon level) have some standardized elements. The objective is for a leader to manoeuvre his soldiers advantageously in relation to the enemy, who may himself be moving or static. The attacker should create superiority in firepower (if not in volume, then in tactical concentration), and aim to outmanoeuvre the enemy by attacking several points at once, thereby continuously throwing the enemy's defence into disarray as he struggles to respond to the tactical complexities.

Here, we will look at fire team/squad level tactics. If the unit comes under enemy fire, the first response is to take cover and return fire while the leader establishes control over all his elements. Most important, he will designate a support group to create a base of fire. This is typically the SAW gunners, who will concentrate suppressive fire upon the enemy, but a modern military force may also have bunker-busting missile systems such as the AT-4 or mortars. In its

US troops practise the most fundamental tactical procedure – fire and manoeuvre. While the troops lying down provide suppressive fire, the other group moves to its next position of cover, before themselves assuming the suppressive role.

simplest scenario, the attack manoeuvre will consist of the support group suppressing the enemy, while the assault group moves in under this cover, using fire-and-manoeuvre tactics to close with the enemy flanks or get around its rear. Note that the quality of the suppressive fire often determines the success of the assault group rushes; if the enemy is able to control its own fire, then the assault team is likely to sustain heavy casualties. Owing to tactical considerations, several additional stages of movement may be required. The assault team and support team together may have to complete several fire-and-manoeuvre stages before closing with the enemy; it is, however, the support element that determines the overall pace of advance.

Naturally, maximum cover and concealment should be used during the advance. In terms of objectives, the attack leaders need to identify weak points in the enemy positions, such as:

● Positions that are badly placed and have poor observation across certain lines of attack.
● Enemy troops who seem to have poor tactical control and fire discipline.
● Covered and concealed flanking routes into the enemy position.
● Exposed enemy supply lines or command posts. These are usually to the rear of the frontline, but circling round the enemy flanks, and attacking these can result in the quickest enemy collapse. (Note that enemy in depth should be targeted by the support fire as much as enemy in

the frontlines. This duty may well be undertaken by supporting artillery and air resources.)

The assault group must close with and destroy the enemy. At close quarters, full-auto small-arms fire and liberal use of grenades are the most effective forms of fire, particularly when clearing out bunkers, trenches or other structures.

Support fire and intelligent manoeuvre must work together coherently for success. Note that support fire has to be rigorously controlled to avoid fratricide. When assaulting an enemy position, for example, the support fire must suppress the enemy at the assault team's entry point, but then switch its fire to other locations as the assault

A bunker attack requires constant suppressive fire to be directed at weapons ports (left), while grenades are used to neutralize resistance in approach trenches.

team attempts to enter that point. Once the assault team is in the enemy position, then support fire should aim to attrit enemy reinforcements or prevent enemy redeployment to meet the assault threat.

DEFENSIVE MANOEUVRES

Defence is often presented as a very passive and static form of tactical manoeuvre, but such is not the case in a professional unit. Defence requires all the planning and activity of attack. In the planning phases, the leader picks defensive positions that maximise CCD, because being undetected is one of the best initial forms of defence. The enemy positions need to be identified, and the defensive positions are ideally located to channel enemy movement into interlocking fields of fire. An ideal location for defensive positions is a reverse slope. This position not only protects the defenders from

enemy observation, it also utilizes the forward slope to soak up enemy fire and makes it hard for the enemy to attack without silhouetting himself on the skyline. In terms of disadvantages, the reverse slope can limit the range of the defenders' observation and grazing fire. Flanking security for a reverse slope defence must be strong.

An alternative to a reverse slope defence is a 'defence in depth' (also known as 'defence in sector'). Here individual units are assigned to defend certain sectors over a wide area, with positions extending outwards in all directions and each unit having initiative in defence of its sector. Each sector will set up its own kill zones, choke points, fields of fire. etc. This set-up is useful for slowing down enemy assaults and breaking up their formations; defensive fire coming from multiple directions leaves the

AL AMARAH ATTACK

On 14 May 2006, a small unit of soldiers of the Argyll and Sutherland Highlanders were conducting a Land Rover patrol through the city of Al Amarah in Iraq. On an exposed highway about 49km (15 miles) from the city, however, they were suddenly ambushed by militia fighters using small arms and RPG (rocket-propelled grenade) fire. The soldiers escaped at speed, but a short distance later came under an even larger ambush and were pinned down. The attacking group numbered around 100 men, some five times larger than the Scottish patrol and supported by mortars. The 20 soldiers dismounted and returned fire in classic anti-ambush procedure. They subsequently, with support from troops and Warrior armoured vehicles of the Princess of Wales's Royal Regiment, turned the defence round to an attack, charging the enemy positions using fire-and-manoeuvre techniques and closing with fixed bayonets. The result was an enemy defeat after a four-hour battle, with 35 Iraqi attackers dead. The British troops suffered no fatalities and no serious injuries.

enemy more vulnerable to strong counter-attack. By contrast, the defenders could opt for a perimeter defence. Here, the unit creates a circular defensive zone, with the reserve, heavy indirect fire support (such as mortars) and command elements in the centre and defensive emplacements ringing the circumference of the position. Ideally, mines and barriers are emplaced around the position. The perimeter format is both its strength and its weakness for defence. The unit will be able to respond to attacks from any angle but, conversely, its defensive power is evenly distributed rather than concentrated at the point of enemy attack.

Basra, Iraq. British soldiers conduct a Land Rover patrol. In hostile areas the vehicle should only be parked where the crew can easily disembark to positions of cover.

Commanders organizing a defence should never think in terms of just sitting and waiting to beat off an enemy attack. A good defence necessarily involves attack. Combat patrols are sent out to interdict enemy supply lines and spoil attack preparations. Artillery fire should be concentrated at troop concentration centres. The defensive positions can act as a decoy to draw out enemy action in preparation for a major flanking attack. If the defence beats off an enemy attack, it must be prepared to counter-attack in force.

One of the most common statements heard from professional soldiers who have been in combat for the first time is that 'the training just kicked in'. The long list of techniques and procedures described above may seem formulaic, but their aim is to give the soldier the correct *automatic* responses in combat, a time when adrenalin and fear often erode the ability to think consciously. That is why soldiers are urged to 'train as hard as they fight', because it is the quality of their training that dictates their ability on the battlefield.

CHAPTER THREE

HEAVY SUPPORT

T he modern infantryman has support resources undreamt of by soldiers fighting in World War II. Close air support, armoured attack and artillery back-up certainly played their part in that conflict. During Hitler's *Blitzkrieg* ('lightning war') operations of 1939–40, the *Wehrmacht* utilized a combined punch of armoured spearheads, aerial bombing, and excellent backup from indirect field artillery to quickly overwhelm their enemies.

However, what has changed is that in modern warfare there is greater precision. Using GPS and laser designators, today's infantryman can bring down first-round fire on his enemy with an accuracy factor of a few metres. Yet, as we shall see, the tanks, artillery and airpower that deliver heavy battlefield support are themselves more vulnerable than ever before.

A US Army M1A1 Abrams Main Battle Tank conducts an area reconnaissance around Balad, Iraq, in 2004. In Iraq armour is used to deny anti-coalition forces the freedom to operate and move throughout the countryside.

ARMOURED SPEARHEAD

In terms of tactical battlefield operations, there are three principal forms of armoured fighting vehicle (AFV): Main Battle Tanks (MBTs), Armoured Personnel Carriers (APCs) and Infantry Fighting Vehicles (IFVs). Examples of the former include the US M1A1/M1A2 Abrams, the British Challenger and the Russian T90. All are characterized by massive specialist armour, a powerful main armament capable of beyond-visual-range kills on other armoured vehicles, and a tracked mechanism that gives them superb cross-country mobility. There are also several varieties of Light Tank, essentially scaled-down MBTs more suited to light combat duties and airborne deployment.

The categories APC and IFV cover a huge number of vehicle types and formats. Both can be tracked or wheeled, and their armament ranges from a simple pintle-mounted machine-gun next to the commander's hatch, through to powerful turret-mounted cannon and anti-tank missile systems. APCs are essentially armoured infantry transporters, typically transporting a full squad or section of infantry. They might also be converted into specialist vehicles, not just simple 'battle taxis'. The Russian MT-LB, for example, can carry 11 fully equipped troops in its simple APC function, but has at least 13 other variants, including the MY-LBU command vehicle, versions fitted with a SA-13 Gopher SAM system or a AT-6 Anti-Tank Guided

The German Leopard 2 is one of the world's most advanced MBTs. Its stabilized gun system can engage targets even while the tank is on the move at speed.

Weapon (ATGW), and the MT-LB mortar carrier, equipped with a 120mm (4.7in) mortar.

IFVs both transport infantry and provide them with heavy fire support once they get to their objective. IFVs such as the British Warrior and the US Bradley and Stryker have demonstrated their value in Iraq and Afghanistan, giving the infantry unit a much greater armoured punch and increased speed and mobility.

The modern infantryman draws on a whole host of other tactical vehicle types, including the lighter vehicles such as the

British Army's Land Rovers and the US forces' Humvees. The most important tactical consideration, however, is that regardless of the vehicle type, its survivability depends upon close cooperation with infantry support.

ARMOURED WARFARE

MBTs are undoubtedly incredible combat machines. The German Leopard 2, for example, can acquire and lock onto targets at up to 10,000m (32,808ft) while on the move, regardless of whether it is night, day or bad weather. With its Rheinmetall 120mm (4.7in) L55 Gun it can then destroy those targets at ranges of 5000m (16,404ft), punching through armour with its depleted uranium

shells. In classic tank vs. tank engagements in open terrain, where enemy infantry resources are spread thin, the MBT can utilize the full range of its speed and power. Here the tactical considerations are much the same as those for infantry – utilizing cover, finding the best fire positions and responding quickly to threats. Cover is particularly important. The tank commander should use terrain features such as hills, valleys and woodland to provide covered movement. When in a firing or defensive position, the tank should ideally be positioned on a reverse slope with just the turret and main gun exposed to the enemy. (After firing, the driver can simply

reverse the tank back down the slope to conceal it from enemy return fire.) For those tank crews with superior tactical movement and the best machines, the effects can be devastating.

Yet tank vs. tank engagements are becoming increasingly rare on today's battlefield. MBTs are still deployed in large numbers, but often in combat situations where a technologically superior army is facing an insurgency force in urban or heavily civilianized environments. We will look more

A Warrior armoured fighting vehicle is guided over a bridge by an engineer. AFVs like the Warrior are becoming essential tools for the safe deployment of patrols in urban settings.

TANK VS. TANK, 1991

During the 1990–91 Gulf War, US MBT forces equipped with the state-of-the-art M1A1 Abrams tank achieved total battlefield supremacy over the Iraqi armoured units. Around 1900 M1s were deployed to Iraq, facing some 2000 Iraqi tanks – mostly T-72s, T-62s and around 700 old T-54s. Despite the Iraqis having superior tank numbers, the M1s totally outclassed the Soviet-era vehicles in every respect, particularly firepower. Iraqi armoured resources were massively reduced by Allied air power even before the land campaign began. The Iraqi army preferred to dig in its tanks as static positions; as a result, precision, air-dropped munitions neatly destroyed hundreds. However, during the land campaign, moving Iraqi tanks were just as vulnerable to M1 firepower. The M1s utilized their thermal-imaging sights to engage the Iraqi armour at beyond visual range at night or during the oil-fire-blackened daytime. Kills were registered at ranges in excess of 4000m (13,123ft). Several hundred Iraqi tanks were destroyed, whereas the US suffered only nine permanent losses and nine repairable losses owing to battle damage (mostly to mines and some friendly fire incidents). Rarely has an armoured engagement been so one-sided.

Although the Cold War has ended, the two recent conflicts in the Gulf have seen tank vs. tank engagements in open terrain, and have proved the superiority of Western armour.

at the specific threats to armour shortly, but suffice to say that the survivability of the tank in these environments depends on infantry support.

Tactical cooperation between tanks and infantry depends on the speed with which the infantry can travel. In the past, troops often went into battle riding on the outside of tanks, but this rarely happens nowadays. Tanks attract heavy amounts of firepower, much of it harmless to the crew inside the armoured shell, but lethal to those outside. Furthermore, having passengers can obscure the tank's vision slits, periscopes and cameras, and interfere with equipment such as smoke dispensers and radio antennae. In today's scenario, the dismounted infantry will patrol the terrain in front of the tank, the whole formation making slow progress at around 30m (96ft) per minute. If the infantry are engaged, they will take cover while the tanks provide heavy return fire with main and auxiliary armaments. A static tank will attract more and more

firepower, so the tank units will usually fall back to predefined defensive positions. The infantry, meanwhile, will engage the enemy infantry and try to destroy threats that the tank cannot effectively engage, such as individual RPG operators working from civilian premises.

The tactical equation changes quite considerably if the infantry have their own armoured transport. Over the last 10 years, it has become fairly standard for infantry to patrol in APCs/IFVs, dismounting only to interact with the locals or to conduct a close-quarters engagement with the enemy. If tanks and IFVs are used together in an attack formation in fairly open terrain, they will typically form several small units advancing in a spaced line. The MBTs will be at the head of each unit as they are much better equipped to deal with and deal out surprise heavy fire.

If the Allied force is engaged at a distance by enemy fire, the infantry will usually dismount at a distance of 500–1000m (1640–3280ft) – beyond the range of much small-arms fire – and advance onto the enemy under the cover of MBT and IFV fire. The infantry should engage the enemy with total commitment despite the presence of armoured support. Enemy combatants will mount a much less effective defence if they are worrying about being killed by advancing infantry as well as by armoured firepower.

While MBTs still have a very important role in contemporary conflict – sometimes just the

The Soviet-era T-55 tank, used by the Iraqi army, was an almost helpless target for Allied ground-attack aircraft and armour during the first Gulf War. Such vehicles could not hide from Coalition surveillance and targeting assets.

appearance of an MBT may cause the enemy to disperse – the vast bulk of armoured combat operations are undertaken by infantry-carrying IFVs. Typically, a platoon of four IFVs will manoeuvre while maintaining around 50m (164ft) between each vehicle. While moving through potentially dangerous areas, several formation options are available, depending on terrain: column, wedge, echelon and line. When stationary, the unit will usually deploy in diamond or opposite-side facing configurations to provide the platoon with 360-degree fire coverage.

Armoured patrol units may be ambushed at close quarters with heavy firepower – this is particularly common in the current urban conflict in Iraq. In these situations the commander must make the decision whether to dismount the infantry

immediately or not. As a general rule, if the fire is coming from all directions – including strikes on the rear dismount doors – then the armoured force should use speed and firepower to punch out of the kill zone to an area safe for dismount, or simple escape. However, if the fire is coming from an identifiable direction, and the infantry can safely dismount in a place with plenty of cover available, then they should do so.

ANTI-ARMOUR TACTICS

As much as infantry need to learn tactical cooperation with armour, they must also learn about the tools and tactics of anti-armour missions.

Almost any modern soldier can have an anti-tank (AT) capability if he has communications; in combat theatres accurate air and artillery fire

A UN forces personnel carrier in Bosnia. An armoured vehicle's windows and vision ports can be some of its most vulnerable points, hence this vehicle's windows are fitted with emergency blast/riot shutters.

is often summoned within minutes of a target being identified. However, here we will look at the personal tools and tactics available to an infantryman to engage armoured vehicles. Note also that our focus here is purely on professional AT weapons, not on the improvised explosive devices (IEDs) used by irregular forces.

The key element of an armoured vehicle that an AT unit must defeat is, naturally, its armour. Armour, both in depth and type, varies tremendously between vehicles. The US Stryker IFV, for example, has ceramic appliqué and steel hull armour that can stop small-arms fire up to 14.5mm (.6in). It is, however, very vulnerable to the rocket-propelled grenades (RPGs) typically used in ambushes in Iraq and Afghanistan, although slot-gap cage armour provides an additional measure of protection. Here, a narrow framework of metal bars detonates an RPG missile before it contacts the main armour, dispersing much of the missile's energy.

For infantry defending against a tank attack, they can take advantage of the tank's limited angle of vision and gun depression at close range. This vulnerability is the main reason tanks must always work in tandem with units of infantry.

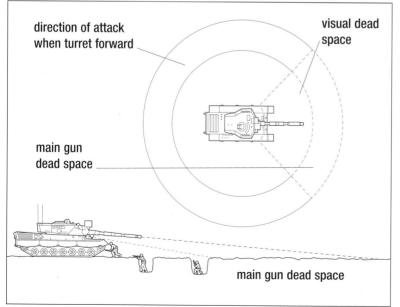

direction of attack
when turret forward

visual dead space

main gun
dead space

main gun dead space

At the other end of the armour scale is modern MBT armour. This itself comes in many different varieties – sloped, spaced, explosive reactive, composite and soft layer – but when done right there is not much it won't stop. For example, the shell that could penetrate up to 1m (3ft 4in) standard homogenous metal armour will not penetrate the 600mm (24in) of sloped

A column of French AMX 10RC move along a road during the first Gulf War. Vehicular columns such as these are very exposed to anti-tank weapons, the lead and rear vehicles being those most commonly targeted.

composite armour found on the US Abrams tanks.

ANTI-TANK WEAPONS

A judicious soldier will match his AT weapon with type of target. For example, a soldier could disable a Land Rover type vehicle fitted with light armour plate with a close-range burst from a Browning M2 machine-gun, yet the same weapon would scarcely scratch the outside of an MBT. The best equipment for any AT mission is a purpose-designed anti-tank weapon (ATW).

The simplest ATWs are shoulder-launched unguided rockets or missiles. The value of

these was first proven during World War II, particularly by the Germans. Panzerfaust-armed infantryman, many with limited training, took a heavy toll on Allied tanks, particularly when firing at ranges of around 25m (82ft) from covered positions in urban or country terrain. Today, the most commonly used unguided ATW is the Russian RPG-7, a staple of terrorist and insurgency organizations worldwide. It fires an armour-piercing High Explosive Anti Tank (HEAT) grenade to a range of 300m (984ft) with a homogenous armour-penetration capability of nearly 406mm (16in). Of similar

capabilities is the Swedish-built AT-4 (now replacing the LAW rocket in US use), which has the same range and penetration statistics as the RPG. Another US service weapon is the Shoulder-Launched Multipurpose Assault Weapon (SLMAW, based on the Israeli B-300), an 83mm (3.26in) weapon used not only for light AT work, but also as a bunker-busting weapon and for use against urban structures. In common with several other unguided ATWs, the SLMAW has a 9mm (.35in) spotter rifle attached. This fires out tracer

Modern anti-armour missiles such as the Javelin automatically make a top attack on heavy armoured vehicles, the missile striking down against the weaker armour situated on the very top of the turret.

rounds that have similar ballistic properties to the missile; when the tracers are on target, the operator will fire the missile.

The advantages of unguided ATWs are that they are usually quick and simple to fire. The main disadvantage, however, is that they can be grossly inaccurate in the hands of an excited or frightened user. After-action reports from Iraq commonly cite numerous RPG missiles being fired at US or British convoys without a single strike. Moreover, the relatively short range and line-of-sight demands of unguided ATWs mean that the user must to some extent expose himself within small-arms range before firing. Many an Iraqi RPG user has been cut down by a SAW burst from his intended target before he

has fired off his missile. Yet one of the main strengths of the RPG-7 is that it and its ammunition are available in great numbers. Consequently, these weapons have caused about 50 per cent of US fatalities in Iraq since the end of the main ground campaign.

ANTI-TANK GUIDED MISSILES

Far better than unguided ATWs are the many anti-tank guided missiles (ATGMs) available. Although generally larger and more complex to deploy, these usually have much greater accuracy, better range and enhanced penetration. ATGMs offer several different types of guidance system. Some (now rather dated) weapons – such as the Tube-launched, Optically Tracked, Wire-Guided (TOW)

missile, the MILAN and the M47 Dragon – utilize wire-guidance technology. Here, the rocket is connected to the launcher during flight by an unravelling wire, and the operator sends flight information down it by keeping the sight trained on the enemy target vehicle.

The key disadvantage of these weapons is that the operators have to stay motionless during the missile's flight, making them a target for enemy small-arms fire. Even those weapons that dispensed with the wire-guidance system in preference for radio guidance had the same problem.

The most up-to-date ATGMs belong to the fire-and-forget class, such as the Predator SRAW and the Javelin. As the fire-and-forget name suggests, here the operator acquires the target and fires the missile, which then tracks the target, leaving the crew free to move.

The lethality of these weapons, even to the heaviest armour, is pronounced. Take, for example, the Javelin. The Javelin operator acquires the target through a Command Launch Unit (CLU), which incorporates a trigger mechanism, an integrated day/ night sighting device and target acquisition electronics. This unit is connected to the disposable launch tube, which contains a 1.76m (5.8ft) long missile with an 8.4kg (18.5lb) HEAT warhead. The missile itself locks onto the infrared signature of the target during the aiming process, and has a range of 2000m (6562ft). When fired against an armoured vehicle, the missile adopts

These illustrations indicate some of the weaker points on Soviet-era armoured vehicles. Good striking points include the joint between turret and hull, access doors and the rear engine compartment.

a top-attack flight profile, ascending to a height of up to 150m (492ft) before diving down on the tank, hitting the typically thinner top armour. Armour penetration is 600mm (23.6in) of rolled homogenous armour. Once the operator has pressed the launch trigger, he is entirely free to move.

TACTICAL CONSIDERATIONS

Such technology makes armour dramatically more vulnerable to infantry on the battlefield, yet the ATW team has many tactical considerations if it is to survive.

First, if the ATW team is armed with an unguided or visually guided weapon, it must know where to target an enemy vehicle's structure for a knockout. Typically, the best locations are:

● Tracks and wheels – an immobilized tank is as good as a destroyed tank in combat terms.
● Engine compartment – engine

ventilation requirements usually require thinner armour here.

● Turret/hull join – hopefully the ATW strike will immobilise turret traverse or allow the HEAT warhead to pass into the crew compartment.

● Crew hatches or doors – applies particularly to IFVs.

● External fuel tanks.

As well as targeting, the ATW operator/crew has to consider all the principles of infantry tactical movement, with an important addition. When any AT weapon is fired, its enormous backblast creates a highly unwelcome visual signature. (The jet of gas is also very dangerous – no friendly troops should be within 30m (98ft) range behind the weapon.) A cloud of dirt and dust is raised high, which will act as a target marker for every enemy soldier in the vicinity. Several of the new missile systems, such as the

The Avenger vehicle is essentially a military Humvee mounted with eight Stinger surface-to-air missiles mounted in two separate pods. The Stinger missiles have a max range of up to 8km (5 miles).

Predator and Javelin, have 'soft launch' capabilities, whereby the missile is blown a short distance from the launch tube by an explosive propellant that in itself creates minimal dust signature, the blast-creating main motor starting up when the missile is a safe distance from the operator. Nevertheless, the AT crew must have covered avenues of escape around their position. They also shouldn't be operating in isolation, and need to receive all the fire support possible from other units.

The ATW crew must also select the best position it can find

to ambush or attack the enemy vehicle. This position must provide maximum concealment while allowing the crew to slip away from the effects of the target's fire if the attack is unsuccessful. The position should also give good protection against infantry responses; the infantry that accompany the enemy tank might actually be the greatest threat to the AT team. Ideally, the AT position should overlook either open terrain, where the tank will be most exposed and the flight of the missile unimpeded, or a confined or narrow route that will impair vehicle speed.

Typical features that slow an armoured vehicle include: walls/embankments more than 1m (3.3ft) high; rivers more than 1.6m (5.25ft) deep; ditches more than 3m (9ft) wide and 1m (3.3ft) deep; slopes steeper than 30 degrees; and any urban or heavily wooded terrain.

If the missile is fired and makes a hit, there are four possible outcomes. First, the attack may be completely ineffective, usually when the missile has not been armed properly or the armour simply deflects the blow. In this instance the AT team should retreat quickly, as the enemy will redirect all available firepower to meet the new threat. Second is a Mobility Kill (M-Kill). Here, the tracks or wheels are disabled, rendering the vehicle immobile

Two US Marines fire a Javelin anti-tank missile in support of operation 'Iraqi Freedom'. The Javelin is one of the most effective anti-tank weapons available today.

ARMOURED SURVIVABILITY

A testimony to the survivability offered to soldiers by armour in the war against an insurgency force comes from the US Army's 1st Battalion, 24th Infantry Regiment. The battalion deployed to Mosul, Iraq, in October 2004 with 75 Stryker IFVs. As with many other armoured units in the theatre, the battalion was subject to almost daily ambush with RPGs and IEDs. In the first six months alone, the battalion suffered 186 RPG, 122 IED and 33 car bomb attacks. Yet the casualties have been kept low thanks to the Stryker's ability to absorb punishment. In a letter

to the *Washington Post*, which addressed controversies over the Stryker's durability, Lt. Col. Michael E. Kurilla, the 1st Battalion's commander, recounted:

I have watched four of 10 suicide car bombs slam into Strykers, creating explosions that are equivalent to 500-pound bombs. One was a suicide truck carrying 52-by-155 mm rounds (a net explosive weight 10 percent greater than a 2,000-pound U.S. guided bomb) that detonated within 25 meters of a Stryker. In all 10 suicide car bomb attacks, not a single soldier riding on

the Stryker lost life, limb or eyesight.

In a further example of the Stryker's durability, Kurilla states:

Over the last six months, one Stryker, C21, has been hit by a suicide car bomb, nine IEDs, eight RPG direct hits and countless small arms. The infantry squad has had six wounded, but every soldier is still in Iraq and still fighting on a daily basis. After each attack, the Stryker continued to stay in the fight or was repaired in less than 48 hours.

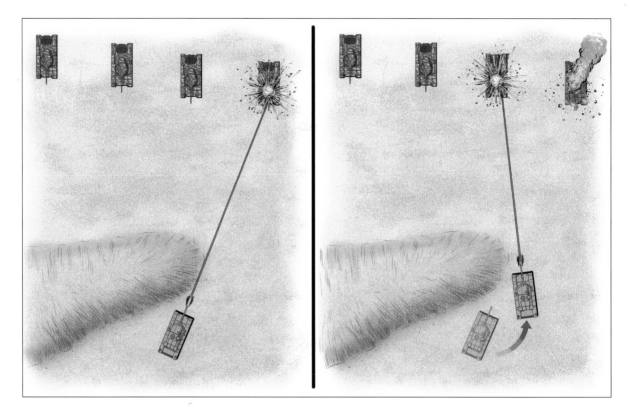

Tanks should utilize cover in the same way as infantry. Here a tank uses a ridge to reduce the advantage of a numerically superior enemy force. By slowly moving around the ridge it can take on the enemy tanks one at a time while retaining flank protection.

but with fully functioning weapon systems. In this instance, the team should redeploy, if safe, to another location and attack the target again or, better still, report the disabled vehicle's location to other armour, artillery and air assets for them to finish off. A Firepower Kill (F-Kill) means that the AFVs weaponry is disabled but it can still move. The responses in this situation are the same as for an M-Kill (even though the weapons are disabled,

the AFV's crew might be radioing in artillery or air strikes against the AT team's position). Finally, there is the K-Kill, denoting a complete destruction of vehicle and crew, the best situation of all.

Note also that an infantry soldier can utilize a friendly tank to destroy an enemy tank, if friendly AFVs are in the area. Once an enemy tank is spotted, the soldier contacts the friendly tank's commander by radio, visual signals or by the tank's external telephone. He then relays target information using the method described in Chapter 1. The axis of arc, however, should be the line of direction in which the tank's barrel is pointing. If the friendly tank cannot be seen, then the soldier can request a ranging shot,

and adjust the fire from the point to impact. Corrections are given simply using commands such as 'left', 'right', 'drop' and 'raise', combined with range adjustment in metres. It is particularly important for the soldier to give full information about the target type – this affects both the ammunition selection and tactical considerations.

SURVIVABILITY

Before turning our attention to the uses of battlefield artillery, it is worth briefly noting ways in which armoured vehicle crews can increase their survivability in places of acute ATW threat. First, vehicles can be adapted to reduce the threat of an ATW strike. Usually this involves placing a structure or object around the most vulnerable parts of the vehicle, including wire cages or sandbags. These have the effect of triggering the missile's warhead before it actually reaches the armour. The vehicle will still be damaged, but the worst of the missile's penetrative/explosive force will have dissipated.

An AFV crew and, in the case of an APC or IFV, its infantry contingent, must have all its firepower ready to counter an ATW threat. As soon as an ATW firing is detected, the area must be saturated in fire. Experience has shown that, particularly with untrained soldiers using RPGs, the firer will often stand and watch his RPG fly to see whether it hits or not.

Many of the operators have been killed at these moments, so the defenders must train themselves not to watch the flight of the RPG but to try, immediately, to target where it has come from. There is even a chance that the small-arms fire may disrupt the guidance efforts of someone using an AT wire or radar guidance system.

ARTILLERY SUPPORT

In an open battlefield (less so in urban warfare), artillery support is one of a soldier's greatest assets.

The Humvee is one of the light armoured workhorses of the US Army. While vulnerable to RPG strikes, it uses speed to escape from ambush situations and can be mounted with many different weapons platforms.

Artillery has several important roles. At its most basic, it destroys enemy personnel and materiel at either a pinpoint or area target (the development of submunition-delivering shells is particularly useful for area targets). The destructive force of modern artillery is truly astounding. For example, during Operation Desert Storm in 1991, a Multiple Launch Rocket System (MLRS) fired a single barrage of submunition dispensing rockets at an Iraqi company. Only 70 out of 250 men were left alive after this horrifying attack. However, there are several artillery functions beyond simple destruction. These include:

Artillery was a central element of US tactics in the Vietnam War. Infantry on patrol would have artillery support at all times from firebases located in remote jungle clearings.

- Fix the enemy in position so that friendly forces can manoeuvre against him.
- Suppress enemy firepower.
- Break up enemy troop concentrations or vehicle manoeuvres.
- Reduce the enemy's ability to manoeuvre around terrain.

The accuracy of modern artillery is astounding, particularly the advent of GPS-guided shells. Prior to this invention, artillery fire would have to be manually guided onto the target by a Forward Observer (FO). The initial ranging shots gave the enemy a chance to find cover and concealment. Today, however, modern artillery can unleash a barrage in which all the initial shells land squarely on the target. Firepower from individual guns has also dramatically increased. For example, the state-of-the-art PzH 2000, a German self-

propelled howitzer, can fire up to 12 shells every minute using its advanced auto-loading system. These shells can make precision strikes at over 40km (25 miles) away; the gun can even fire five shells in decreasing elevation, resulting in all five of the shells striking the target simultaneously.

MORTARS

At the other end of the scale, however, is the infantryman's own personal artillery – the mortar. Depending on the type of weapon, mortars can hit targets ranging from 100m (328ft) to in excess of 25km (15.5 miles), although up to 3.2km (2 miles) is more common. They also fire a variety of practical ammunition types: high explosive for anti-personnel/materiel effects; obscuration rounds such as smoke or white phosphorus to provide visual cover, or to mark a target

for heavier air or artillery assault; or airburst illumination rounds.

Mortars have several advantages for the infantryman over heavy artillery. First, a mortar is highly portable and can be emplaced in seconds on just a few square feet of ground. This gives it an immediate response role; it can take many minutes sometimes to call in a heavy artillery strike. Second, a mortar's high angle of fire means that it can operate easily from behind dense cover, or even within woodland.

During the Vietnam conflict, US Special Forces teams would use light mortars to strike Viet Cong/NVA positions even in the thickest jungle, firing up through holes in the jungle canopy. Mortar shells also have a steep angle of drop. Whereas a conventional artillery shell might come in at a shallow angle and impact on upper tree branches, a mortar shell is much more likely to drop down through the foliage to reach the enemy beneath. Finally, mortars carry a respectable above-ground lethality, because the slow rate of drop prohibits the shell burying itself deep in the ground before detonating.

For example, a 60mm (2.36in) high-explosive mortar round can kill in a 20m (66ft) radius from the point of impact. It is for reasons such as these that during the British Burma campaign in 1945, infantry units replaced most of their anti-tank guns with 3in or 7.5in mortars.

Mortar emplacements can be either improvised on the spot or established in pre-prepared positions. US firebases in Vietnam

would often ring the perimeter with mortar positions. A good quality mortar pit is dug deep and wide enough to give a mortar unhindered fire over the rim and allow it a 360-degree traverse, while protecting the crew from small-arms fire. Although mortars can be placed almost anywhere, there are some ground-quality requirements.

The soil should be well drained and solid to prevent the baseplates sinking in under recoil and therefore affecting the

French UN troops set up a battery of mortars in the former Yugoslavia, 1995. The firepower and range of the large-calibre mortars, as well as their superior portability, often obviate the need for reliance upon heavier conventional artillery pieces.

mortar's accuracy. Conversely, frozen earth can result in the mortar making a dangerous slip when it is fired. In this case, the mortar team cuts slots into the ground into which the baseplate spades are fitted.

MORTAR ACTION

In June 1944 Company C, 39th Infantry Regiment, US 9th Infantry Division was advancing against enemy positions at Cherbourg, France. Suddenly, the company's 1st and 3rd Platoons came under massive enemy fire, which consisted of machine-guns, 88mm (3.46in) flak guns, field artillery and some German mortars – the longer-range weapons began to strike the 2nd Platoon that was following up to the rear. The US troops were pinned down, and an attempt at a flanking manoeuvre ended in failure with heavy casualties. Company C then called upon its own weapons platoon, which was armed with three 60mm (2.36in) mortars, plus

the firepower of 81mm (3.18in) mortars used by the regiment's heavy weapons company. The mortars began laying down constant fire upon the German positions. Although the enemy was not entirely neutralized by this fire, his casualties were heavy and much of his firepower was suppressed. Over several hours this allowed the infantry to close up once more to the enemy, eventually overwhelming the German positions. Afterwards, Company C's commander credited the mortars not only with aiding the eventual victory, but also in preventing Company C from being wiped out by enemy fire.

A soldier from the 101st Airborne Division sprints for cover after his position comes under mortar fire. Mortars are priority targets for an enemy, and so will quickly attract counter fire as soon as they are identified, often from other mortars.

Because mortars are so portable, however, there is the danger that fire missions will be rushed and can endanger friendly forces. So, mortar fire should be strictly controlled along the following guidelines. Note also that these guidelines apply to controlling artillery fire in general, not just mortar fire.

PRE-PLANNED MISSIONS: Pre-planned fire missions are usually part of an organized attack or defence. Each artillery unit is given strict grid coordinates that control the permissible target area, demarcated by fire lines and fire areas. The fire lines establish a line in front of which the mortars must not fire, while the fire areas are specific geographical targets into which the mortar may fire. Note that today's highly mobile battlefield means that the fire lines and fire areas are frequently changeable, and the mortar unit must be fully briefed on the fire-sequence timetable.

HASTY MISSIONS: Hasty mortar fire is usually called in by a designated FO or a soldier acting as such, in response to combat developments. More about controlling artillery fire in general is described below, but the FO will have to understand the limitations of the mortar. Mortars are rarely able to achieve the type of wholesale destruction that an MLRS or PzH 2000 is capable of, so the FO must only call mortar fire on those targets a mortar can suppress for long enough to allow an infantry unit to make a new manoeuvre.

Another consideration for both an FO and a mortar team is survivability. Like a machine-gun, a mortar is a priority target for the enemy. Mortars generally have much less of an auditory and blast signature than conventional artillery pieces, but that does not make them undetectable. Professional armies now utilize counter-artillery and counter-mortar radar systems to give precise locations of enemy

artillery. For example, the US Lightweight Counter-Mortar Radar (LCMR) tracks the flight of mortar shells through 360 degrees of the radar unit emplacement, feeding data back to the unit's command and control centre via a wireless link. When enough data is collected – and this can be achieved with only one or two rounds of enemy fire – the grid coordinates of the mortar are plotted, and can be fed directly to counter-artillery fire batteries or Close Air Support (CAS) assets. Not all armies have such technology, but a mortar remains highly vulnerable to enemy responses.

There are several measures a mortar crew can take to improve survivability. Overhead cover will necessarily be limited, as mortars fire upwards, but as many as possible should be in place to mask the crew from an aerial surveillance. Like a machine-gun team, the mortar team should not fire its weapon constantly if close to the enemy.

Bursts of rapid fire followed by a break will not only make the mortar harder to detect by auditory means, but will give the mortar tube time to cool and so reduce its thermal signature. Another survivability measure is the use of shoot-and-hide

A US 81mm (3.19in) mortar is readied to fire. In the hands of an expert team, a mortar can fire as quickly as rounds can be dropped down the tube. However, this advantage also requires extremely careful discipline with ammunition consumption.

positions. Here, the mortar crew fire from one position and hide in another when not firing. During the hide periods, the mortar can either be left in place or the base plate left in situ to allow quick reassembly of the mortar in the correct firing position. GPS-programmable mortars make shoot-and-hide actions more convenient, as the mortar is immediately brought back on target once it is reassembled. Alternatively, the mortar team can simply fire from several different positions in order to confuse enemy detection.

When the enemy is employing counter-mortar radar, the mortar team can respond by reducing the ammunition charge and lowering the angular trajectory of the mortar shell. Both of these measures reduce the amount of time the shell spends in flight, giving the enemy radar less time for detection. Furthermore, the lower angle increases the chance of radar confusion as the shell stays closer to ground terrain and features. Note also that mortars rarely fire alone. If several mortars are used, they are usually positioned in a staggered relationship, with plenty of distance between each tube. Changing the sequence in which the mortars fire can also confuse enemy detection procedures. Of course, one of the best aids to mortar survivability is close infantry cooperation. Mortar teams need to make sure their mobility matches an infantry advance or withdrawal – they should not be isolated from main forces.

FIRE DIRECTION

Controlling artillery fire is one of the more specialist infantry skills. It is also a great responsibility; many a soldier has been killed by his own artillery following an errant fire-control order. Secure and clear communications between the FO and the artillery unit must be established for a fire order to be successful. Furthermore, in British and US forces, soldiers are always taught to write down their fire order on paper before broadcasting it. This stops the soldier having to think while on air, and so reduces the risk of mistakes.

The first stage of a fire mission order is simply to alert the Fire Direction Centre (FDC). This is done by stating an identification, saying 'fire mission', then 'over'. The FDC should then confirm that they are ready to receive the fire mission. Now the FO must designate the location of the target. The simplest method for doing this is simply to give grid coordinates. The soldier can consult his map and plot the target on this. Range-finding and GPS equipment can also provide distance information for the FO, but if this is not available,

A typical mortar position. Note how the sandbag perimeter is placed far enough away from the edge of the hole to allow soldiers to fire small arms with their elbows supported on the ground.

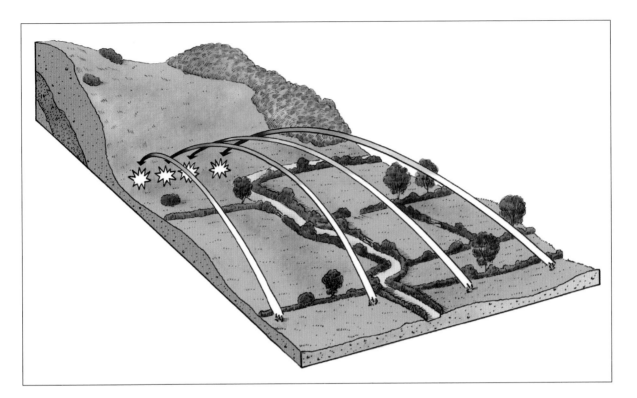

then the FO will probably have to give a direction to the target from his own position. He gives the distance to the target and the angle from his position in mils. There are 6400 mils in a full circle, and military optical instruments (such as binoculars and telescopic sights) and compasses often have these marked up in 10-mil increments. (Some optics will also feature basic distance-finding gradations.)

If these aren't available, the fingers can provide a rough mils calculation. With the hand at arm's length, the fingers' width gives mils as follows:

    1 finger – 30 mils
    2 fingers – 70 mils
    3 fingers – 100 mils
    4 fingers – 125 mils
    5 fingers – 180 mils
    Spanned hand – 300 mils

Once the soldier has distance and range figures, or a target grid reference, for the target, he must also warn of any proximate friendly forces. There should be at least 600m (1969ft) distance from friendly troops and exploding mortar fire, rising to 2000m (6562ft) for very heavy artillery types (such as naval gunfire or MLRS strikes). The soldier then needs to describe the type of target. This is particularly critical, as it affects both the artillery's ammunition selection and its fire pattern. Targets are described in terms of equipment and action (e.g. 'tank firing from dug-in position'). They also need shape and length descriptions.

A battery of mortars will position themselves ideally with a distance of 300m (984ft) between each tube to provide protection against counter-battery fire.

This particularly applies to area targets, e.g. an enemy ammunition dump which is 200 x 300m (656 x 984ft), because a target that is more than 600m (1969ft) long in any one dimension will need more than one artillery piece to tackle.

With the target located and described, the FO then recommends the type and duration of fire. Commands for types of fire can include 'neutralize', 'smoke', 'suppression' and 'fire for effect', which will give the FDC a good idea of what is required. The FO must always remember,

AS90 guns from engaged Iraqi positions as they support the battlegroup of the 1st Royal Regiment of Fusiliers outside Basra. Self-propelled guns such as these are in many ways taking priority over towed artillery in modern armies.

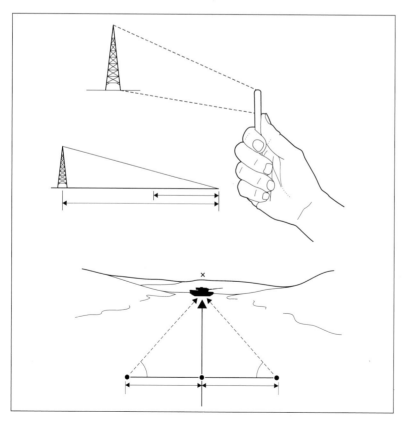

however, that other units may have a claim of the artillery resources, and ammunition expenditure must be kept to a minimum.

Usually, just enough fire is provided to suppress the target, sufficient to provide the infantry with a manoeuvre opportunity. To accomplish this, the soldier may give a time duration for the bombardment, or observe the fire and give a cease command when the intended effect is achieved. He may also stipulate start and stop times for the fire order, when he wants to coordinate the fire precisely with an attack or defence manoeuvre.

Once the FO has given all relevant information to the FDC, he makes the request for fire, and observes the fall of the initial

An artilleryman or forward observer can use simple principles of triangulation to calculate the height of distant objects or the distance to that object from the observer's position.

rounds. Unless the artillery makes a precision GPS strike, the shell fall is unlikely to be bang on target with the first rounds. The FO must therefore adjust the fire on to the target. First, the soldier corrects the target line by simply stating 'left' or 'right' and giving the distance in metres. Then the FO must correct for range, using the 'bracketing for range' technique. This works in the following way. If the first shells fall short of the target, the FO then corrects the fire so that it, in his estimation, falls the same distance long of the target. The FO then subdivides the distance, alternating short and long (or vice versa, depending on the initial shell drop), and so shortens the distance from the target until shells are falling precisely where intended.

Once the artillery shells are directly striking the target, the FO will then state 'on target' or 'fire for effect', at which point the artillery will deliver the full firepower requested in the initial fire order. When the target is destroyed or the fire has accomplished the objective, the FO will signal 'end of fire' to complete.

DEFENCE AGAINST ARTILLERY

As much as it is vital for an infantry soldier to be trained in controlling artillery, it is equally important that he knows how to respond when trapped by artillery fire. A soldier's primary objective under indirect fire is to remove himself from the killing area as quickly as possible. This can be easier said than done. If the artillery fire strikes heavily,

suddenly and accurately, the most immediate response is to get down into substantial cover as quickly as possible.

Preferably this cover should be below ground level, such as a ditch or pre-dug trench, as this will be best protected from the effects of shrapnel. Ideally, a soldier should also grab some overhead cover as well, as airburst shells may be used. A simple expedient can be simply crouching under a flak jacket.

If there are breaks in the artillery fire, or the fire is slowly being adjusted onto target, the soldier and his unit should run

US Marines fire an M198 Medium Howitzer while providing supporting and defensive fire for Camp Fallujah in Iraq, 2004. With rocket-assisted projectiles its max range is 30km (18.6 miles).

US Marines in a well dug-in position on a ridge take cover from Communist mortar fire during the Korean War, January 1950.

or crawl out of the killing area. Shellfire often precedes an infantry attack, so it is important that the unit moves together to retain unit integrity in case it needs to mount a defence. While escaping the artillery bombardment, at least 10m (33ft) should be maintained between individuals.

At night the unit must be prepared to respond to enemy illumination tactics, which can be a prelude to indirect artillery fire or some other form of attack. There are two types of flares: ground flares and aerial flares. The moment a ground flare ignites, the unit should quickly move out of the lighted area and find cover – ground flares are

SHELLFIRE EFFECTS

In a study of infantry psychology during World War II, artillery and mortars ranked as the most feared types of weaponry, greater than machine-guns, dive-bombers or high-altitude bombers. The principal reasons for this fear were the accuracy of the attack and the lack of warning. The devastating effects of shellfire are apparent in this letter from the previous world war, written by the Australian infantryman John Raws on the Western front in the summer of 1916:

For a while I am attached to an entrenching battalion, consisting of fighting men temporarily engaged on engineering enterprises along the front. From what I can see, the infantry spend five out of every six hours at the front in various labour of this sort – building up, repairing and pulling down here, there and everywhere, and carrying, carrying, carrying sandbags, timber and earth from morn till eve, and then till morn again. And all the time a very remorseless enemy plugs us whenever he can see us and thinks it worthwhile. Almost always we are hidden from his guns, but they have countless eyes aloft and all our anti-aircraft guns and our own aeroplanes cannot keep them always closed. So gunners, way back behind the German lines, who have never seen us and our works, peer over maps all covered with little squares, and then turn handles, squirt out wonderful little instruments giving levels and directions, and then, pipe in mouth, just press a button or pull a string, and away comes a little token across the sky to us. We hear it coming with a great nasal screech, and if it gets louder and louder we just flop down in the mud, wherever we are, and pray or swear, according to our individual temperaments. Mostly, however, they don't trouble about small working parties, preferring to devote themselves to observation posts, high buildings, main roads and gun emplacements.

often tripwire triggered, and the enemy will have his weapons trained on to the area around the flare. If an aerial flare is launched, the soldier should simply hit the ground and lay flat, preferably while the flare is rising, when it will not be at full illumination. Bright flares tend to iron out colour contrast in the terrain but heighten shadows, so movement stands out more than shape.

AIR SUPPORT

Air support is now one of the most important additions to infantry firepower, both in terms of combat and logistics. Two aspects have become especially important in terms of tactical movement: calling in CAS and manoeuvring around the battlespace by helicopter.

Helicopter transport provides a unit infantry with an extra dimension of travel and tactical options. It allows for rapid vertical envelopment of a target, fast medevac facilities, point-specific resupply in remote locations, wide area search-and-rescue capabilities and also heavy fire support from an attack helicopter. A typical helicopter-based mission is an aerial assault insertion. Like any aviation operation, this requires intense planning. The planning phase in the US military takes into account seven major considerations:

GROUND TACTICAL PLAN: This is the overall mission plan for ground operations, which dictates all aspects of the deployment from arrival at the landing zone (LZ), mission objective and extraction.

FIRE SUPPORT PLAN: If helicopters are flying into potentially hostile

A US Army Special Forces Humvee awaits a Black Hawk medical helicopter at a rendezvous point in southern Afghanistan, June 2004. The LZ is well selected, with a good approach and a flat landing area.

SMALL ARMS AGAINST A FLYING TARGET

When firing small arms at a moving aerial target, there are three methods of lead adjustment. First is changing lead. Here, the gunner fires at a certain distance ahead of the aircraft and attempts to maintain this lead by swinging his gun along the flight path. The fly-through technique, by contrast, involves several gunners shooting at a fixed point in the sky (often marked above a tree, aerial or other salient feature) through which the aircraft will fly, hopefully incurring damage as it does. Finally, the pattern-of-fire technique involves several gunners using the changing lead technique, but all having a different lead pattern to maximize the chances of a hit. The type of technique is selected according to the number of men firing and the time opportunities to organize the unit.

Pakistani soldiers carry tents away from a US Army CH-47 Chinook helicopter during a humanitarian mission. The Chinook is a powerful supply tool for ground forces, with a lift capability of over 9000kg (20,000lb).

LZs, the landing site or the ground troops' routes of deployment may be prepared with artillery fire. The helicopter pilots must plan their flight paths to avoid flying through outgoing fire or touching down at an LZ when fire support opens up.

LANDING PLAN: The landing plan designates the precise location of the LZs (primary and alternate), the time of landing, and the sequence by which different elements of the helicopter force will land. (For example, combat elements will usually land first to secure an area, allowing for logistics sorties to fly safely in later.)

AIR MOVEMENT PLAN: This part of the planning process dictates how the helicopter flight will move from departure point to LZ and back again. Considerations here include flight altitudes, routes, formation and speed. Most importantly, the air movement

plan should provide the safest route of travel, bypassing or quickly overflying enemy positions, using terrain cover in potentially hostile areas (such as flying through valleys).

Weather conditions also have a major effect on the air movement plan and, in fact, every other stage of the planning phase. Adverse weather can severely limit a helicopter's capabilities, so should be avoided if necessary.

LOADING PLAN: The loading plan dictates how personnel and equipment will be loaded aboard the helicopters for the mission. This has critical mission implications. If landing in hostile areas, for example, it is probably best for SAW gunners to disembark first to establish covering fire – hence they must get onto the helicopter (depending on the helicopter type) last. Squads and fire teams should travel together in one helicopter to preserve tactical integrity at the battlezone.

The principal unit commanders, however, should be split between helicopters so that if one helicopter goes down, it

British troops unload their kit from a Chinook helicopter after landing in Helmand province. An unloading plan needs to be developed before soldiers disembark, and the landing area will also need to be secured by advance forces. Also, kit that is required for immediate defence must be put aboard last during the loading phase.

doesn't take out the entire mission leadership.

STAGING PLAN: This is principally focused on the selection of, and procedure at, pick-up zones (PZs) once the mission is completed.

APACHE AH-64D LONGBOW

The Apache AH-64D Longbow is an exceptional aerial asset for supporting infantry units, particularly against enemy armoured vehicles. It is now the US Army's main attack helicopter, and is also entering service with the British Army. Every inch a frontline helicopter, it can operate in almost any weather condition, night or day, utilizing an ultra-sophisticated Target Acquisition Designation Sight, Pilot Night Vision System (TADS/PNVS).

This incorporates a thermal imaging infrared camera, a monochrome daylight television camera, a laser range finder and a laser target designator, all slaved to the pilot's head-up display (HUD)

unit. The AH-64D's prominent Longbow Fire Control Radar also allows the pilot to detect and engage enemy vehicles even when the helicopter body is hidden behind terrain. In terms of armament, the Longbow packs 1 x 30mm (1.18in) M230 cannon and outboard wing stubs that can carry AGM-114 Hellfire anti-armour missiles, AIM-92 Stinger and AIM-9 Sidewinder air-to-air missiles, and 2.75in Hydra rocket pods. In combat since the first Gulf War of 1990–91, the Apache has proved itself to be an efficient armour killer, albeit one unexpectedly vulnerable to simple ground-to-air fire from infantry.

The staging plan incorporates many of the planning phases above, particularly the loading plan and also the coordination of fire support resources.

The selection of appropriate LZs/PZs is critical to the smooth running of any helicopter operation. Not just any patch of ground large enough to take a helicopter will do. Understanding landing areas is critical to infantry in case they must find an improvised PZ for an emergency extraction. Firstly, the landing area must be big enough to give plenty of space for the helicopter's rotors, and this varies according to the helicopter.

A UH-1 or AH-1 assault helicopter requires 35m (115ft) diameter of landing space, while a large cargo helicopter such as a Chinook needs 80m (262ft). The

space considerations are also affected by approach/departure requirements.

Approach/departure routes should be free from obstacles (such as trees, radio masts, large hills, etc) and should allow the helicopter to fly into the prevailing winds straight into the long axis of the LZ/PZ. A simple formula helps the soldier determine whether a height obstacle affects the usability of a landing area. The US Army's *Ranger Handbook* (SH 21-76) gives this formula as follows:

For planning purposes, an obstacle clearance ratio of 10 to 1 is used on the approach and departure ends of the PZ or LZ. That is, a landing point requires 100 feet of horizontal clearance if

a helicopter must approach or depart directly over a 10-foot tall tree. A lesser ratio may be used if the helicopter executes a steep approach or departure in emergency situations or with light loads.

Deciding to use lesser ratios of approach/departure depends on the judgement of the pilot, who will have final say in such matters.

Note, also, that when a helicopter has a near maximum capacity load, its obstacle clearance ratio will increase above the norm and it may not be capable of a vertical landing/lift-off manoeuvre.

Regarding the physical conditions of the LZ/PZ itself, it should be relatively flat and free from potentially damaging obstacles such as tree trunks or large rocks. Note that a covering of snow, sand, dust, etc can obscure ground obstacles.

If a unit is marking out an LZ/PZ, obstacles are indicated with red panels during the day and red lights during the night. The landing point's earth must be firm, with good rainwater drainage. Most importantly, in a combat situation soldiers should choose an LZ/PZ that has the least likelihood of enemy presence.

If possible, soldiers appropriately mark out the LZs/PZs for approaching helicopters using ground marker panels or lighting. Furthermore, there is a full range of arm movements used to control the helicopter's flight in and out. For example, both arms raised directly above the head means 'this way', holding the arms out horizontally to the side means 'hover', while the arms crossed and extended downwards in front of the body signals that the helicopter should land.

ASSAULT EMBARKATION

For an infantry unit, helicopter embarkation and disembarkation is governed by a set of particular rules. A squad of infantry will be placed into a 'chalk' unit before boarding a helicopter, with an NCO in charge. He ensures that the squad is properly configured for helicopter flight: radio antennae are down, kit is properly secured and the men are appropriately lined up to board the aircraft (in single file, and fulfilling all the conditions of the loading plan). Only when given permission by the pilot or crewman does the chalk embark aboard the helicopter.

Disembarkation can be a very different experience from embarkation, depending on the reception faced at the LZ. As the helicopter touches down, all personnel evacuate the cabin and fan out to positions 15–20m (49–66ft) around the helicopter. There they lie prone with weapons at the ready until the aircraft has departed the LZ. If the enemy engages the helicopter during the landing – what is known as a 'Hot LZ' – the troops

An Apache helicopter, here stacked with AGM-114 Hellfire missiles, is a considerable anti-armour threat. The Hellfire has an 8km (5 miles) range and is also used as a bunker buster.

follow the same disembarkation procedure, but immediately return fire. Essentially, the Hot LZ is treated with basic anti-ambush tactics, the purpose being to escape the LZ area, which the enemy is treating as a kill zone. Note that the helicopter, or other attack helicopters, will often make attack passes over the LZ in an attempt to suppress the enemy prior to landing. Typically, these involve steep angular dives in which the helicopter drops from around 492m (1500ft) to 164m (500ft), unleashing a pattern of rocket and machine-gun fire while on the dive. It will usually then bank away sharply, avoiding overflying the target where it is most likely to be exposed to

upcoming anti-aircraft (AA) fire. When the time comes for the unit to be picked up following their mission, security measures around the PZ must be especially tight. Full CCD measures – particularly light and noise discipline – should be employed on the approach to the PZ. At the PZ, one group will establish all-round security at the PZ perimeter, while another group prepares the PZ for helicopter deployment (removing obstacles, laying out marker panels, etc.).

CAS – ATTACK

Close Air Support (CAS) consists of air-to-ground strikes in support of ground forces manoeuvres. It is a highly complex process

involving as much planning by aviation assets as infantry soldiers, so our study of it here is far from exhaustive. Through the parallel development of precision air-dropped munitions and equally precise target designation systems, CAS has become one of the soldier's greatest assets on the battlefield, one that even threatens the rationale behind artillery and armour. In Iraq, for instance, CAS aircraft responding to emergency calls have saved both British

A typical helicopter attack run using unguided missiles involves a 10–30-degree dive at the target from altitude of around 492m (1500ft). The helicopter should not overfly the target, as here is likely to be the heaviest AA fire.

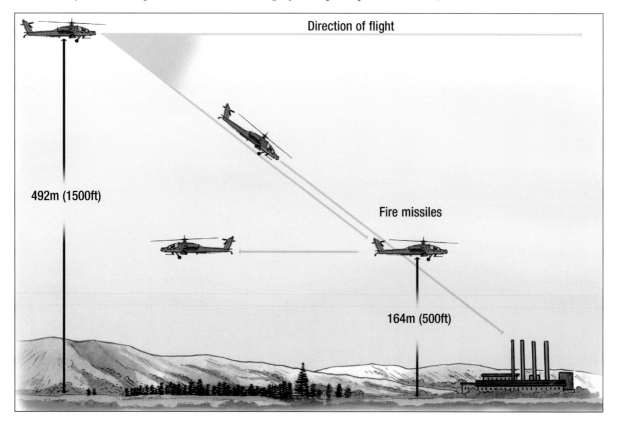

Direction of flight

492m (1500ft)

Fire missiles

164m (500ft)

The A-10 tank-buster aircraft's principal weapon is the devastating 30mm (1.18in) GAU-8/A Avenger Gatling gun, which can fire at a rate of 70 rounds every second. Because it has a relatively slow speed, the A-10 is heavily armoured, the pilot sitting in a titanium 'bathtub'.

and US forces lives. For example, AC-130 Spectre gunships, which carry a devastating combination of 20mm (.8in), 40mm (1.57in) and 105mm (4.13in) cannon, have at times put down precision fire on insurgent positions within 100m (328ft) of Allied soldiers, to devastating effect. (The motto of one of the AC-130 squadrons in Iraq is: 'You can run, but you'll only die tired.')

However, there is a danger of thinking of CAS as an easy resource to call on. Good CAS requires first-rate planning, technical understanding and, above all, communications. Bad CAS is just as hazardous for friendly forces as for the enemy. For a pilot flying at 4500m (15,000ft), the view of the ground has none of the clarity possessed by ground forces, which can lead to tragic mistakes. Modern air-dropped munitions are also enormously powerful, and care has to be taken to put soldiers out of the blast radius.

Essentially, there are two types of CAS: planned and immediate. Planned is a pre-planned air-support operation, usually prepared several days

before a major operation. Immediate CAS is, as the name suggests, an unplanned call for air support from infantry units based on the unexpected events of the battlefield. Both must rigorously control the distance between friendly troops and the aerial attack. This is either accomplished by a ground controller feeding target information to the attack aircraft, or by the establishment of a Kill Box. The Kill Box does not, strictly speaking, belong within the category of CAS. A Kill Box is a three-dimensional area of the battlespace in which air assets are freely able to locate and attack targets. Note that while the Kill Box is planned in detail, usually by a Joint Force commander, pilots are able to initiate attacks within the Kill Box without further coordination.

There are two types of Kill Box in US tactical thinking. A Blue Kill Box allows any air-to-surface fire without ground-fire coordination. A Purple Kill Box is the same, but allows for coordination with ground fire (although still without headquarters consultation), hence

bringing an element of CAS into the equation. The most important points about a Kill Box is that all ground forces assets in the battle space know its precise location, and the controlling headquarters moves or cancels the Kill Box according to the minute-by-minute tactical situation.

PROCEDURE

Within the context of immediate CAS, there is a fixed procedure for calling in an air strike. First, the controller (the infantryman requesting the CAS) makes contact with a known air asset using the aircraft's call sign, and confirms his own identity. The controller will then define the type of air support required (usually by code number) and designate the start point for the attack run, giving full coordinates. Next, the pilot receives details of the target location in relation to the start point, including heading in degrees, distance, the target elevation in metres above sea level, the target description and finally the target location. The target location is described through grid coordinates, longitude/latitude or visual

An Iraqi vehicle column lies wrecked in the desert in 1991. Most of the Iraqi vehicle losses were inflicted by Allied air power.

reference, e.g. 'tank parked by side of X bridge, east side of Y river'.

Sometimes this will be enough to direct the attack aircraft to the target, but in today's battlefield the target will frequently be marked by technological means, either to give the pilot a visual reference or to provide direct guidance for precision munitions. The target can be marked most crudely by a white phosphorus munition, but laser, infrared designators and GPS targeting systems give pinpoint precision. To prevent precision-guided

munitions (PGMs) coming into conflict with multiple designation signals, the controller will give the pilot a code that locks him onto the controller's specific target information.

As the final parts of the CAS briefing, the controller provides the location of friendly troops (particularly their distance from the intended target), instruction about egress from the attack point, information about enemy presence and also the Time on Target (TOT), the time at which the munitions are expected to strike. Once everything is clarified, the controller gives the pilot clearance to drop/fire.

Clarity is indeed the watchword of a successful CAS mission. If at any point the controller

gives incorrect information, he should clearly state the word 'wrong' and give the correct information.

CAS – DEFENCE

For those soldiers who are the victims of CAS by modern fixed-wing aircraft, the defensive options are fairly limited. As with responding to artillery fire, the unit should attempt to move as quickly and inconspicuously as possible out of the kill zone. Putting up heavy amounts of anti-aircraft (AA) fire rarely brings down an aircraft, particularly if it is making a low-level pass. So, during the early stages of Operation Rolling Thunder (1965–68) – a massive US air interdiction campaign against North Vietnam during the Vietnam war – more aircraft were lost to conventional AA than to North Vietnam's highly sophisticated SA-2 Guideline missile network, primarily because of a risky, low-level strike strategy. The military has, since then, responded appropriately, and on most occasions CAS aircraft will be deployed above effective AA range.

Of course, advanced surface-to-air missile systems are available, such as the US man-portable Stinger and the advanced Patriot system. Because the US forces generally establish air superiority wherever they go, there has been little call for such systems in combat. However, they are extremely accurate, and a good SAM missile network can present a major problem for attacking aircraft, if not in terms of

actual losses, then certainly in terms of disrupted accuracy. The normally dominant Israeli Air Force (IAF), for example, suffered heavy casualties against Egyptian SAM batteries during the Yom Kippur war. The Egyptians built up an extensive network of Soviet-built SA-2, SA-3 and SA-16 missiles, with a result that whereas in the Six-Day War of 1967 the IAF lost only 26 aircraft, in 1973 115 aircraft were downed (according to Israeli figures, though some credible estimates put the figures much higher).

Although a fixed-wing jet is extremely difficult to down by a normally equipped infantry unit, a helicopter presents a much more viable target. Helicopters are slow moving and low-level aircraft

with extremely poor flight characteristics if the main or tail rotors are damaged. Helicopters operating over urban terrain, especially if they are hovering, are easily intercepted from rooftop fire positions. Consequently, during the infamous 'Blackhawk Down' incident over Mogadishu, Somalia, in 1993, untrained terrorists firing RPGs at close ranges shot down two US Blackhawk helicopters. Apache helicopters flying over the former Yugoslavia and over Iraq suffered some critical damage at the hands of small-arms fire, and this has forced a major tactical rethink of assault helicopter operations.

To engage a helicopter, a soldier should find a position of good cover but with clear fields of fire over open skies or down

The loss of two Blackhawk helicopters in Mogadishu in 1993 was a shock to advocates of US airpower. The helicopters were simply shot down by unguided RPG fire.

common flight channels (such as valleys). Full auto fire is concentrated towards the pilot cabin, the engine and main rotor, and the rear tail rotor. The soldier should not expose himself for long, however. If the helicopter is armed it can make a very powerful and accurate fire response in a matter of seconds, so the soldier should fire a concentrated burst, then quickly redeploy himself undercover. Whether attacking or defending, any soldier should have a healthy respect for support weapons, whether they are airborne or not.

CHAPTER FOUR

TACTICAL TERRAIN

I n the distant past it was possible to train only to fight on 'home' terrain or to expect an enemy to choose a suitable place for a battle, which would likely be fairly open terrain. This is no longer the case: modern forces may be sent anywhere in the world and may have to contend with jungle, grassland, mountain, arctic or urban environments.

Experience has shown that while motivated and well-led troops can adapt to almost any circumstances, the learning curve tends to be steep and littered with the bodies of comrades. Thus it is necessary to train for these environments even if combat in them is not expected in the foreseeable future.

THE EFFECTS OF TERRAIN AND CLIMATE

Terrain has always been a factor in warfare. The ancient Persians were known to smooth out the ground they intended to fight on, in order to give their chariots a better run at the enemy. Leonidas and his 300

'You fight like you train, so train like you want to fight' – armed with M16A1 automatic rifles, US Army officers practise making good use of terrain on the Infantry Officer's Training Course.

Spartans could not have made their epic stand on open terrain – the enemy would have walked around them – but in a narrow mountain pass they were able to stall a much greater force until betrayed and flanked.

Accounts of historical battles tell us much about the use of terrain. The more-or-less accidental use of dead ground by Prussian cavalry approaching the French lines at the battle of Gravelotte/St-Privat negated the advantages of the long-ranged Chassepot rifle. The woods at Agincourt channelled the French cavalry into the English archers' killing ground, and the 'hedgerow hell' of the Normandy *Bocage* (farmland

An infantry force disperses by squads to set up a defensive position along the hedge line. The machine-gun teams are widely separated to give interlocking fields of fire.

criss-crossed by trees and hedgerows) allowed Allied tanks to be ambushed at close range.

Terrain is a neutral factor in that both sides can exploit it. Making effective use of the ground is a vital skill for combat troops and their commanders, and most armies train in specific tactics to take high ground, make use of woods and so forth.

Climate is also a factor. Troops unused to hot conditions are quickly fatigued by high temperatures and casualties due to heatstroke are not uncommon. Extreme cold can cause weapons and vehicles to malfunction, and of course can kill poorly protected troops. There are also psychological factors involved with climate.

Heavy rain predisposes troops to seek shelter from it and stop moving, to hunch up and look down. Cold saps morale very

quickly and troops who are overly concerned with staying warm tend not to be effective even if they can be induced to leave their shelters at all.

Then we must consider the obvious physical hazards of climate and terrain. Snakes, floods, tropical diseases, rockfalls, crevasses, glare-blindness and simply getting lost are all hazards the modern soldier must contend with while trying to find and defeat his enemy.

DESERT WARFARE
World War II in the North African theatre was to a great extent a 'gentleman's war', fought mostly in the open without complications such as civilians getting in the way. The desert does favour the sort of fast-moving, hard-hitting operations that modern armoured formations, backed up by aircraft, do best.

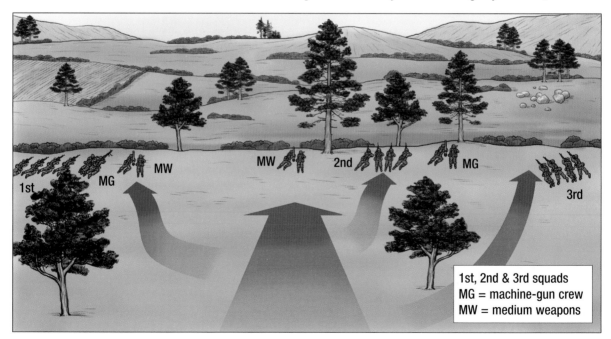

1st, 2nd & 3rd squads
MG = machine-gun crew
MW = medium weapons

Although dusty conditions are tough on hardware and vehicles, the desert is in many ways the ideal terrain for tanks and other combat vehicles.

The two main problems with desert warfare are navigation and logistics. The former is much easier nowadays with the advent of the Global Positioning System (GPS) and its general availability. Logistics, however, remains an issue.

Troops functioning in the desert need all the usual things – ammunition, food and fuel – but also greater quantities of water than normal. Precautions against climactic hazards also include eye protection (from glare as well as dust or sand particles) and suitable clothing. Heatstroke and severe sunburn are ever-present hazards.

Manoeuvring in the desert is not usually much of a problem for troops using vehicles unless soft sand or rocky areas are encountered. The main problem is that enemy observation is very easy. Dust plumes can be seen from a great distance and there is rarely much to conceal a deployment or advance.

Although it is possible to see a very long way in the clear desert air, rangefinding can be a problem. Objects often seem to be closer than they actually are, and heat haze can distort images or even refract light sufficiently to create a 'ghost target' or mirage. An elevated position is useful, since looking down on the target eliminates most of these problems. It is worth noting that optical devices such as laser

US Marines moving on foot in Afghanistan. The desert is an unforgiving environment where unprepared troops can become casualties without ever coming into contact with hostiles.

rangefinders and binoculars are fooled as easily as the human eye in these conditions.

In addition to heat and glare, the desert offers a number of hazards. Soft sand and areas of dunes can be entirely impassable to vehicles, and sometimes to humans on foot. Rocky areas are not uncommon, sometimes with steep hills or mountains. These

can be quite large and often create natural strongholds with only a few easily defended paths up to the top.

Water, ironically, is a serious hazard in the desert. Seasonal lakes and rivers can seem to have dried up but remain soft and damp underneath the surface, potentially trapping vehicles that attempt to cross them. Flash floods, caused by heavy rainfall somewhere else, can threaten troops using dry riverbeds to move around.

Of course, the most well known threat in the desert is the sandstorm. Nothing can be done amid one, except to find some kind of shelter and wait it out. The airborne sand gets into everything, making even breathing a problem. Engines and equipment need to be protected as much

A soldier of the French Foreign Legion well covered up against dust and sand during the First Gulf War. The Legion is expert at desert warfare and maintains specialist training centres to maintain its capability.

as possible, and weapons or equipment that have been exposed will need cleaning before they are used.

OPERATIONS IN THE DESERT

Infantry operating in desert terrain will almost always be in conjunction with vehicles. Objectives are likely to be water sources, natural strongholds in rocky areas or else centres of population, including towns, oil wells and so forth. Anyone defending these places is unlikely to be surprised, so the emphasis must be on speed and firepower to overcome the defenders before casualties mount.

If local conditions allow, air and artillery support can be used very precisely in the desert, and it is difficult (but by no means impossible) to conceal positions from air or satellite reconnaissance.

The desert is thus in many ways a fairly simple environment to fight in. Providing the logistics tail can provide sufficient water and fuel, combat operations are a matter of advancing rapidly to contact and deal aggressively with the enemy. There are relatively few difficulties with locating the enemy in such an open environment and close-range ambushes are difficult to stage. This means that vehicle-borne

troops can get quite close to the target before deploying, although this in turn renders them vulnerable to long-range fire.

ARCTIC WARFARE

Arctic terrain is in many ways similar to the desert. Glare and temperature (in this case low rather than high) can disable troops who are not adequately protected. The most serious problem in this environment is, of course, preventing frostbite and debilitation due to the extreme cold. Good clothing is vital, but so is the training to use it properly.

Simply piling on as many layers of clothing as possible is all very well, but this can restrict movement to the point where the

soldier is unable to operate effectively. There is also the risk of actually becoming too warm. Sweat-soaked clothing conducts heat away from the body rather than insulating it.

The risk is greatest when troops must move fast or engage in heavy activity and then stop or take cover. Overheating while rushing to a new position, then crouching in it, slowly becoming chilled is not conducive to combat effectiveness. Troops must therefore know how to use their clothing, and the clothing must be flexible enough that they can adjust the amount of insulation to suit their conditions.

The old adage that 'if you lose your gloves, you lose your life' is

Japanese Ground Self Defense Force (JGSDF) soldiers practise their skiing skills. Crossing snow-covered terrain is greatly facilitated by using skis.

very true. It does not take much to stop a man's hands from working properly in cold conditions, and once that happens the soldier will need assistance or he will be in very serious danger. Hats and hoods are also vital; heat loss through the head is tremendous. People will often take off their hat if they are too warm. It is better, however, to loosen the coat and leave the hat in place to avoid frostbitten ears and excessive cooling.

Cold presents problems for equipment, too. Some electronic

A traditional solution that still works; these Austrian soldiers can lead their sure-footed pack ponies into places that most vehicles simply cannot go.

equipment must be kept warm to work. Lubricants become thick in cold conditions, and fuel may not ignite in an engine. Rubber tyres can perish and plastic objects can become extremely brittle. Frozen water in vehicle radiators and pipes will wreck an engine. Even metal is not immune to the effects of temperature; weapon components can fail due to cold or through the rapid heating from extreme cold that is experienced when firing. Moving through arctic conditions poses a number of problems. Snow is hard work to slog through and skis need training before they are useful. Vehicles can get stuck in deep snow, which also conceals all manner of hazards such as uneven terrain, rocks and the occasional crevasse.

Ice can cause problems, whether underfoot or forming on objects. It is only slippery down to a certain temperature (depending on what is passing over it), as the slickness comes from a layer of melted ice caused by pressure. At low enough temperatures a man's weight will not cause the surface ice to melt, and thus not cause slippage.

However, melting ice is particularly dangerous. Not only is it slippery but it can also conceal liquid water underneath. Falling through ice can be fatal for a man; even if he is not lost under the ice and drowned, he may die of hypothermia from the cold.

ARCTIC COMBAT OPERATIONS

There is not much to fight over in the arctic wilderness, so arctic military operations tend to centre on the protection or capture of important targets such as population centres, industrial sites and so on.

Effective use of camouflage is important in arctic combat. Terrain tends to consist of rock, snow/ice and forest, so obviously a predominantly white camouflage is best. Pure white is actually fairly easy to spot, so dark objects such as weapons are not the liability they may seem.

The main feature of arctic combat is that everything takes longer, and usually involves more personnel. A good position may seem just a short rush away, but getting there through heavy snow can take much longer (and be far more tiring) than it seemed at first, granting the enemy more time to shoot, resulting in correspondingly higher casualties. Weapons need to be kept out of the snow as much as possible.

Throwing a recently fired rifle into a snowdrift might result in a warped barrel as it cools rapidly, and any moisture picked up will freeze on the weapon at the first chance. Rapid cycles of heating and cooling are not good for any material.

MOUNTAIN WARFARE

Mountain environments can be very harsh. High altitudes tend to be very cold and exposed to high winds and snow or rain, and getting around is a problem. Terrain is usually steep and sometimes impassable except by slow climbing that leaves personnel vulnerable to attack. What good routes there are will usually be known to the enemy and under observation.

Two points may not be very far apart as the crow flies, but travel between them can be a lengthy process when they are separated by a valley, ravine or difficult terrain. On the other hand, it may be totally impossible to see an area that is actually quite close, leading to the possibility of moving into an ambush or unexpected encounter.

There is also the problem of altitude. Not only is it cold at high altitude but the air is

'Bullet drop' can make aiming a problem, but in some terrain it is an asset. This support gunner is aiming above the target area and dropping his fire onto it, allowing him to hit distant, concealed targets.

STORMING THE FORTRESS

Insurgents operating in Oman in the late 1950s had access to a formidable natural fortress in the Jebel Akhdar, a high rocky region with very limited access. Removing them would be a difficult undertaking.

The breakthrough came when an SAS party gained access to the Jebel by a route thought by the rebels to be impassable and thus unguarded. The achievement is particularly remarkable in that the SAS men led an unlikely assortment of other troops to the top, including engineers, signalmen and medical corps soldiers, plus a group of vehicle crewmen from the Lifeguards whose vehicles had been disabled by mines. Some of these soldiers were very recent recruits.

The Lifeguards lugged nine .50-calibre machineguns dismounted from their vehicles up the Jebel, and with their support the SAS team were able to storm a key rebel position, laying the groundwork for eventual victory.

also thinner than at sea level. 'Altitude sickness' is essentially an inability to get enough oxygen to the body and brain in order for them to function properly. This can lead to troops becoming tired quickly if unacclimatized and can cause confusion or slow responses to dangerous situations.

Mountain roads are perfect for ambushes. Often overlooked at many points, they are usually narrow, twisty and not very good, forcing users to travel slowly, allowing hostiles to fire down from their positions. Often ambushers can strike and then fade away long before reinforcements reach the scene.

MOUNTAIN COMBAT OPERATIONS

Combat operations in mountain (or even just hilly) terrain are difficult to undertake. Mountainous areas are often impassable to vehicles and make support by artillery and aircraft problematical. The main problem, however, is having to think in three dimensions.

As already noted, distances are effectively multiplied by difficult terrain and most positions

The wrong and the right ways to place sandbags on a slope. Constructions (A) and (B) are unstable, while (C) and (D) are arranged securely in a horizontal plane.

are overlooked by somewhere higher. Getting at enemies occupying such an overlooking position can be a problem; many times troops have fought their way to what they thought was the summit only to find another ridge beyond and enemies firing down from it.

Mountain warfare is essentially positional. An advance must be conducted in leapfrog fashion, with troops positioned to give covering fire if necessary while another group moves towards its new goal. Once the new position has been occupied, the covering force can in turn move up. This requires patience

and tenacity, especially if the terrain is very difficult or the troops are required to carry a lot of gear.

Assaulting a defended position in mountains is a very dangerous business. Troops struggling uphill through difficult terrain and prepared fields of fire are at serious risk unless the defenders can be heavily suppressed.

Many mountain campaigns have been won by a flanking manoeuvre, often using an unlikely or highly dangerous route, but one not covered by the enemy, to gain a positional advantage in turn.

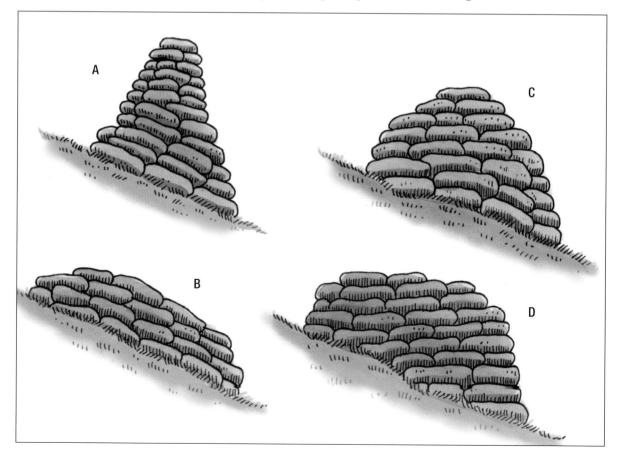

JUNGLE WARFARE

Jungle is perhaps the ultimate in 'close terrain'. In some areas it is not possible to see more than a few paces in any direction and movement speeds can be measured in kilometres per day. Jungle poses severe mobility problems to vehicles and restricts them to roads, which are not usually very good.

However, jungle also conceals the movements of troops and is less of an obstacle to those who know how to move through it. As the Allied defenders of Singapore in World War II discovered, it was relatively easy for Japanese troops to infiltrate past their positions and attack from behind. Allied thinking was wedded to the concept of controlling the roads and fighting a set-piece action against enemy forces. The Japanese were not willing to play this game and caused mayhem with the Allies' plans.

Visibility is a problem in jungle, as is the fact that there is always noise and movement to distract and intimidate troops. For those not used to the jungle it is a frightening, hostile and oppressive place where it is easy to get lost, and ambush could be just seconds away. Soldier

US troops in Vietnam. One of the main problems encountered by US troops during this conflict was not hitting a target so much as locating one, and tactics had to be adapted accordingly.

confidence is vital in such an environment, especially when friendly troops may be close by

TIME AND DISTANCE

It is not distance that separates places, but the time taken to get from one to another. Fighting in New Guinea in World War II, Australian and Japanese troops exchanged fire between fortified positions on two neighbouring hills. No part of either side's position was more than 400m (1312ft) from the other, and in places the gap was only 150m (492ft). Rifle, mortar and machine-gun fire between the two positions were constant but indecisive.

An inexperienced Australian officer suggested sending a force to assault and remove the Japanese position. The idea was rejected on the grounds that while troops in the two positions could shoot and even shout insults at one another easily enough, the terrain in between was so bad that an assault would take an estimated three weeks to get into position to attack.

By comparison, the Apollo missions went to the Moon and back in an average of 10–12 days.

but out of direct contact. The possibility for disaster is increased when troops become nervous.

In addition to impairing contact and visibility, jungle terrain imposes many obstacles on weapons fire. Trees and bushes will stop a bullet, and any branch will send a thrown grenade or even a mortar bomb bouncing in an unintended direction. Fire support can be a problem as rounds will sometimes detonate on contact with the jungle canopy, and correcting the aim of air or artillery support is difficult for observers who may not be able to see landmarks or even tell where shells are coming in.

The jungle environment is hazardous, especially for those who did not grow up there. Poisonous insects and snakes combine with tropical diseases to create a risk for all personnel going into the jungle. Over time, any force deployed on jungle operations will suffer attrition and casualties due to these factors. These can be kept to a minimum by vaccination and by learning about the jungle so that soldiers are able to live in it rather than simply crash through it in search of targets to shoot at.

A hilltop defensive position in jungle terrain. The trenches are positioned to cover the most convenient avenue of approach, the gully.

PENETRATING THE JUNGLE

Gurkha Lance-Corporal Rambahdur Limbu won the Victoria Cross for his actions in combat against insurgents in Indonesia. Limbu was a Bren gunner whose team-mates were killed by enemy fire. Thinking he might be able to save them, Limbu carried first one and then the other to safety over open ground under machine-gun fire, then went back for his weapon and stormed the enemy position alone, destroying it.

The insurgents were dug in on a hill in thick jungle, and the only way to get close enough to attack was to cut a path though the jungle with secateurs. The Gurkhas' scouts accomplished this without being detected, and the force was able to crawl up to within striking distance. The jungle that provided such an obstacle also covered the Gurkhas' approach and allowed them to launch their attack from close to the enemy.

COMBAT OPERATIONS IN JUNGLE TERRAIN

The key to good jungle fighting is to fight the enemy, not the jungle. Troops need to be able to move through the terrain and make use of it without being intimidated by it. This requires familiarity with the jungle and also confidence in other members of the unit.

Combat in the jungle is characterized by sudden and often fleeting contact with the enemy, and there is rarely any time to organize a complex plan or bring up reinforcements. Thus troops need to be able to respond to a threat aggressively and flexibly without relying on close control. It is vital that everyone knows what to do in an ambush or sudden contact; support weapons must be brought into play as quickly and effectively as possible, and enemy troops need to be suppressed by heavy fire.

Good scouting and security are a vital part of the jungle combat equation. Contacts often occur at close range and the side that has the most warning has the advantage in this situation. Where the enemy cannot be clearly seen, 'reconnaissance by fire' is a viable tactic. By shooting into an area, it is sometimes possible to determine if there are enemies present – they will either shoot back or decamp quickly – even if they are not eliminated. Enough firepower can clear foliage away and expose enemies hiding behind it, though usually they will be hit or chased away before this happens.

Interdiction is a useful jungle warfare tactic. One method is to drive the enemy into a known area and then saturate it with artillery or air-delivered firepower, or to force an enemy unit to retreat along an obvious path that has been mined or is set up for ambush. A variation on this is to airlift troops in behind an engaged enemy force, which is either attacked from the rear or runs into the 'anvil' when it attempts to withdraw. The British in Malaya successfully used this tactic.

Observation of likely enemy routes allows ambushes to be set up, especially if the hostiles have predictable habits. Another trick is to set up an ambush and do something that draws forces into it. For example, an outpost might be attacked to draw a rescue force out. As this force hurries along a predictable route, it can be ambushed or shelled. A force that can be induced to run into a minefield can be cut up badly for a very small investment on the part of the attacker.

US infantry training in Jungle Warfare techniques in Okinawa, Japan.

AMPHIBIOUS OPERATIONS

Amphibious operations are among the most hazardous of military undertakings. Boats or vessels are very exposed when close to the shore and have limited room to manoeuvre if they come under attack. Beaches and riverbanks tend to be open areas that must be crossed in order to get to or from the landing vessels. The key to successful amphibious

US Marines go ashore from a Landing Craft Utility (LCU). Getting across a defended beach is a dangerous business; troops are burdened with equipment and sand is tough going. Also, there is little cover on a beach.

operations is to have the correct assets available and a good plan for using them. It is hard enough to put a combat force (of any size) ashore and support it there without discovering that vital assault supplies cannot be landed quickly for lack of landing craft or helicopters.

Similarly, if stores are going to be landed, then they must be stowed in a logical order. Bad logistics can cripple an operation, and there is no excuse for having to move tentage and spare clothing to get at ammunition while the amphibious force is trying to hold the beachhead. Good reconnaissance is vital, and all the

more so if large vessels are involved, as major ships are extremely vulnerable close to the shore. Shallows, deep channels, mined areas and other hazards must be known about in advance if the operation is to have any chance of success. Any enemy defences must obviously be reconnoitred, and if possible the means to neutralize them should be built into the plan.

Response times for enemy reinforcements, and the routes they will take to the combat area, are useful to know. If a responding force can be interdicted or at least attrited on its way to oppose the landing, the chances for success

US Marine Corps amphibious vehicles approach the beach. Vehicles offer a measure of protection but more importantly can carry supplies and fire support weapons up the beach and directly inland.

will increase considerably. Close cooperation between services is also necessary, which means exercising together. Compromises have to be made. For example, the best opportunity for an air attack to suppress enemy defences may have to be passed up if it will take away the element of surprise from the main assault. The same is true of a strike to take out enemy air assets on the ground if the aircraft are already in the air and attacking the landing force.

'HOLD OR ABORT'

One vital factor in an amphibious operation is the inclusion of a clear 'hold or abort' policy, which requires good, fast communications between everyone involved. It may be necessary to postpone an operation for minutes, hours or days due to unexpected events, or to abort if it seems that the enemy is prepared to meet the attack. Several tragedies have ensued from operations that, once begun, rolled onward into the teeth of increasingly heavy odds because there was no easy way to abort them.

Logistical support is vital in most cases. A special-forces raid from boats or a submarine might be a simple in-and-out matter, but most other operations have to be supported once in place.

This requires a steady flow of resources, which must be transported and protected. Similarly, supplies must be protected once landed.

Actually getting ashore presents a number of problems, which can be minimized by good reconnaissance. At one time the only feasible way was to run shallow-draft assault landing craft (LCA) ashore and rush up the beach.

Today there are more options: helicopter or tilt-rotor craft flying from landing ships can land troops inshore in what is termed an 'over-the-beach' assault. Hovercraft, small boats and amphibious vehicles can all be used to transport troops onto a beach quickly and protect them as they push inland.

COUNTERATTACK

A counterattack of some kind must be expected. Initially, it may be disorganized and composed of those nearby forces that react quickest, or it may be an air strike on the landing force. In fairly short order, however, enemy forces are going to make a serious and organized attempt to remove the lodgement, and the ability to defeat this counter-attack will determine the success or failure of the mission. This means that the landing force must have the support of anti-tank and anti-aircraft weapons if it is coming to stay – if the plan is just to make a quick visit then these are less critical.

Getting back off the beach may also be a part of any operation. Withdrawal is an expected part of raiding operations, but a failed amphibious assault will also require extraction, often under increasing pressure. Heavy fire support must be used to suppress enemy troops, coupled with good organization that allows units to pull out coherently. The operation must be carried out under cover of a rearguard confident of escape and therefore motivated to stand their ground until it is time to withdraw. Amphibious retreat is one of the most fraught of military operations but it must be planned for, just in case.

AMPHIBIOUS COMBAT OPERATIONS

Amphibious operations can be quite minor, a matter of slipping a small force ashore to carry out reconnaissance or sabotage, or to gather information. Such operations can be stealthy affairs

that the enemy never even becomes aware of, let alone opposes. Major operations or invasions are harder to conceal and tend to meet some kind of resistance.

If resistance is met, then fire support is of the utmost importance. It may take the form of naval bombardment, tactical air support or direct-fire weapons aboard the vessels – or all three – but whatever its form, the support must be prompt, heavy and on target.

Speed is vital, but simply rushing up the beach is unlikely to succeed. Once military forces become disorganized, their capabilities plummet, and blind haste will shatter organization. Instead, an amphibious force must be able to advance quickly without losing cohesion or contact

with supports and friendly units.

Combined arms cooperation is vital to overcoming enemy defences. Ideally, this will take the form of heavy firepower directed by forward observers or air-liaison officers, but on a smaller scale the ability to coordinate support fire from a unit's machine-guns or grenade launchers with infantry manoeuvre is equally critical.

Aggressive tactics are the only way to succeed in an amphibious operation. There is little cover to be had on a beach or riverbank, and becoming pinned down will lead to slow elimination. The only answer is to deal with enemy strong points and move inland, and this requires the ability to advance confidently even under fire.

More than anywhere else, good planning and clear objectives are vital. The assault force needs to establish a lodgement and eliminate any immediate threats to that area, such as support weapon positions overlooking it. This allows follow-up forces to arrive unhindered and begin their advance. The force can then gradually widen their 'bridgehead' and remove threats as combat engineers clear obstacles. This must be done in a coherent and logical fashion and may require close cooperation between units of different types.

Only when a beachhead has been secured can the assault force move inland. It is usually necessary to clear a wide area around the landing beach and defend (or at least observe) it

Assault amphibious vehicles driven by US Marines from the 31st Marine Expeditionary Unit make their way towards the well deck of the amphibious dock landing ship USS Harpers Ferry *(LSD 49) in the Gulf of Thailand, May 2006.*

to prevent harassment from unsecured flanks.

The landing beach is a vital lifeline for forces ashore and the area between units operating inland and the supplies arriving at the beach is an artery that must be kept open for the duration of the operation. This corridor is also the line of withdrawal for the force and needs to be secured in case a quick exit is necessary.

AIRMOBILE OPERATIONS

The air is not a combat terrain for infantry as such, but air-mobility is used to get into and out of most other combat environments. It imposes certain considerations in addition to those implied by the terrain to be fought over.

Airmobile operations are little more than a half-century old, but they are extremely important in modern warfare. Airmobile troops can bypass enemy defences and difficult terrain to strike at their objectives, and can achieve surprise by arriving at their target in minutes or hours, whereas a ground force would take much longer, if it could get there at all.

Early airborne forces were very much one way, arriving by parachute or glider. Resupply was usually only possible by air or by forces advancing to link up. Paratroops (and glider-borne forces) were useful in an advance in that they could arrive suddenly on an objective ahead of the assault and take it by surprise, for example at the Eben Emael

Chinese marines, supported by amphibious tanks, drive ashore during an exercise in 2005. Firepower and a rapid advance off the beach are the keys to victory.

fortress in Belgium or in the unsuccessful operation Market Garden, where paratroops seized key bridges ahead of the main force, which was unable to effect a link-up.

Paratroops could also be dropped in the path of an enemy advance to slow it down and buy time, though in the words of one ex-Para this tactic would result in 'thirty minutes of confused but furious resistance followed by a massacre. We were to be an airmobile speed bump'. More usefully, paratroops could land

Airborne deployment into water is a relatively new technique and is only used in special circumstances. These soldiers are USAF Pararescue personnel – everything they do is special.

behind an enemy advance and try to disrupt the logistics chain, theoretically acting as an 'anvil' that the enemy is driven back onto by the 'hammer' of a counter-attack. More likely the paratroops would be dispersed, short of supplies and quickly mopped up after making a brief but serious nuisance of themselves.

ONE WAY ONLY

The problem with parachute and glider troops was that they were

one way only. Extraction was virtually impossible, so they had to win, be supported or be lost. Supplying airborne troops is a problem. For example, during the German invasion of Crete in 1941, some paratroopers landed in 'hot' zones carrying only a pistol, and had to go looking for their rifles, which had been dropped separately. Resupplying the invasion force was a major problem.

The advent of true airmobile forces changed all this. Using helicopters (and tilt-rotor aircraft) for both mobility and as fire-support platforms, airmobile troops can strike hard and fast, and can be sustained in their field by the same helicopters that delivered

them. Casualties can be extracted by air and the entire force can be pulled out the same way. Airmobile troops no longer need to conquer or die.

However, helicopters are not fast and are vulnerable to small-arms fire when flying low, and especially on the ground. They cannot operate without some measure of protection from enemy fighter aircraft, and while they can and do land in 'hot' landing zones, this leads to losses among expensive aircraft.

One problem with airmobile operations is that of environment acclimatization. Troops go straight from their base to the combat area, which can lead to unfamiliarity with, or detachment from, the environment, resulting in mistakes or weakening morale. On the other hand, the chance to return to a relatively comfortable base in the rear rather than slogging overland to combat, with all the dangers inherent in such movement, is a bonus to many military units.

AIRMOBILE COMBAT

The key to successful airmobile operations is to strike by surprise, using heavy firepower to overcome local opposition and to keep the enemy off balance. The 'indirect approach' expounded for mobile armoured forces applies even more to airmobile troops. It is not easy to guess where a helicopter-borne force might be headed as it loads up, and misdirection can be added to the mix

by air strikes in support of a fictional airmobile operation somewhere away from the intended target. In many cases the enemy might have no idea a strike is coming.

Airmobile operations have much in common with amphibious combat, in that they require good planning, clear communications and good cooperation. Airmobile operations tend to be of short duration and the transport assets must often remain in proximity to the combat area. Flight time is limited, which raises the question of whether to return to base, to stay in the landing area or to retire to a safe 'laager' somewhere nearby. Laagering is a risk of course, and requires a secondary force to secure the area and avoid attack

by nearby enemy ground troops. Approach to the landing area should be made low and fast, with support available from fixed-wing aircraft or heavily armed gunships to suppress enemy forces in the immediate area. Troops need to get out of the helicopter and into defensive positions or some kind of cover as quickly as possible, covering all possible angles of attack. This is important whether the landing zone is 'hot' (i.e. under fire) or not; all-round security is vital even if no threat is expected. Troops are most

While some observers suggest that the traditional parachute insertion is outmoded, these Indian paras continue to train for it just the same. Once on the ground, troops are a lot less vulnerable than on the way in.

vulnerable when moving from the transport into cover, so this needs to be accomplished quickly but without losing contact with one another. Rehearsal and good training allows a unit to debus quickly and efficiently. As with amphibious operations, immediate opposition needs to be dealt with either by ground assault or supporting assets.

Once on the ground and secure, the airmobile force can advance against its objective. In some cases this might be immediate, such as when a

force makes an assault landing directly onto the objective but, more commonly, some ground movement is necessary. Speed and aggression are the order of the day. Troops undertaking this kind of operation usually have the advantage of going into action rested and knowing what to expect.

A pre-mission briefing can include the most recent data in whatever detail is necessary. However, there are always surprises and these must be overcome quickly before the enemy can recover.

WITHDRAWAL AND EXTRACTION

Once the objective is captured or eliminated, or if the force gets into difficulties, withdrawal and extraction can be a tricky business. As with an amphibious operation, fall back to the extraction point must be in a controlled and logical manner, with good support from gunships, artillery or whatever other support is available. It may be necessary to launch short counter-attacks to prevent enemy forces from organizing, and these must not get out of control. 'Mission creep' could result in a rearguard force getting too far from the extraction point and into difficulties.

It has been known for airmobile forces to have to fight their way to the extraction point (or an alternative one), and this poses severe problems. The morale of troops who think their mission is over, who are tired and perhaps low on ammunition, bringing casualties with them, can sometimes be very brittle. Good training and the elimination of expectations can help here. The Samurai adage, 'when the battle is over, tighten your helmet straps', is very apt here. For the airmobile soldier, the mission is not over until he reaches base, and relaxing before that, however understandable, is to court disaster.

US and Iraqi troops dismount from a C-47 Chinook helicopter during Operation Swarmer in March 2006. Airmobility offers huge advantages to a force trying to combat insurgents hiding out in remote areas.

RIVERINE OPERATIONS

Rivers offer an easy way to move around, especially in heavily forested or jungle terrain. However, they have a set of hazards all their own. Obviously, there is danger from shallows and rapids, and from local wildlife. Piranha, crocodiles and snakes could potentially devastate a military force without any enemy action.

Close terrain (e.g. jungle) along the river line can conceal a large force with quite heavy weapons. This can make river patrols less effective, as there is a limit to what they can see but, more importantly, it can hide hostiles until they strike.

The main threat to riverine operations comes from the riverbank. Rivers are, by definition, fixed in their course and there are few alternative routes. If a force is using boats, its route can be predicted, and that makes an ambush easy to stage.

However, river patrol craft can mount heavy weapons and, in some areas, they are the only way to move support weapons and supplies through difficult terrain. The supply routes must be kept open, so combat patrols are necessary despite their risks.

When the German light cruiser *Konigsberg* took refuge in the Rufiji river in Africa during World War I, she was inaccessible to the

A British Combat Support Boat (CSB) off Basra, Iraq, in 2006. Small boats permit mobility along coastlines and waterways, but they are very exposed in open water so constant vigilance is essential.

Allied forces in the area. It was necessary to undertake an extensive riverine operation (with naval gunfire and seaplane support) to get at her. In the end she was defeated by shallow-draft river monitors, which were pushed upriver despite heavy resistance from the banks. This opposition had to be cleared by troops operating from the boats in an environment they were not trained for nor experienced in.

RIVERINE COMBAT OPERATIONS

If contact with the enemy occurs it will take one of two forms. Hostile or suspicious vessels may be encountered and searched or dealt with. Alternatively, vessel-to-shore action may take place.

In either case, combat will be short and very violent. Troops will have to fight from where they are with little chance to manoeuvre or seek cover. There will be no chance to run ashore and engage the enemy closely or find a good position. If the vessel affords no real cover, then there is none to be had. The only chance is to eliminate or suppress the enemy force before it can do too much damage. This is especially important with inflatable boats, which do not cope well with combat damage.

Action against another boat involves a clear target, allowing deliberate marksmanship, but in the case of an ambush or combat with enemies on land, heavy automatic fire is necessary to suppress suspected enemy positions. Support weapons must be targeted as a priority and dealt with before they can cripple the unit's vessel.

A version of standard anti-ambush drill is necessary, using a massive response to drive the enemy under cover as quickly as possible. If it seems possible to tackle the enemy directly, then fire support can be called in and the unit might close with the enemy. If not, then a quick retreat is called for – there are no halfway measures when under fire from the bank. Generally, a combat between boat and shore will be

Urban terrain is three-dimensional and very complex. Troops can move on the ground, above it or under it, changing levels to fight or escape at need. This can be a nightmare for troops not familiar with the area when fighting those who are.

decided fairly quickly. Either the ground troops will cripple the vessel, with very heavy losses to those aboard, or else they will be smothered by return fire and forced to retreat. External factors such as reinforcements or even artillery support will usually arrive too late to affect the outcome. By the time they take effect, either the riverine force will be winning or it will be well on its way to defeat.

URBAN OPERATIONS

In truth, conflict can happen anywhere there are people, and people, of course, are always to be

found in cities. Urban combat is becoming ever more common, and urban terrain is the most difficult to fight in. This is partly because of its nature – plenty of cover and ways for hostiles to move around unseen – and partly due to the risk of collateral casualties.

The capability of the best modern forces to dominate the open battlefield tends to be a factor in driving enemies into the cities. Facing an enemy with command of the air and excellent artillery and armour support, the less well-equipped opponent must seek some way to neutralize these advantages. Urban areas offer all the advantages of other close terrain such as woods, and, in addition, the presence of civilians places limits on the use of area-effect weapons. Urban combat is a difficult, unpleasant business, but it is the future of warfare.

The urban environment is cluttered with obstructions to visibility, especially for troops moving at ground level. A sniper who intends to remain static for a long period can get up into a high place where his field of view (and fire) is better, but for the mobile patrol this is not an option. One solution to this is to position observers or snipers up high to protect the patrols, but this takes time and personnel that simply may not be available.

Most of the visual obstruction will also provide cover from small-arms fire. Troops cannot shoot at what they cannot see, but even a known target can be difficult to hit, especially if it is under cover. On the other hand, missed shots tend to ricochet around the urban environment, as there are plenty of hard surfaces for them to glance off. This can pose a hazard to troops and non-combatants. Most hard cover will stop shell and grenade fragments, but fragments of stone or brick can be dislodged in their turn, creating an additional danger.

CHOICE OF COVER

The choice of cover is thus something of a problem. Ideally, cover should consist of something that will stop a bullet without showering the soldier with

fragments, and provide maximum concealment without impeding his observation or field of fire. One case in point is using a car as cover. Most parts of a car can be considered concealment rather than cover – the bodywork will not stop a bullet, but the engine block will. Firing over a vehicle from close to it (e.g. in the so-called 'barricade position') can be dangerous. A missed shot might ricochet from the bonnet or roof up into the soldier, so it is sometimes better to stand a pace or two back from the vehicle rather than close up against it.

There is little in the typical city block that will stop a heavy

machine-gun round. A .50 calibre machine-gun will chew through most buildings in short order, and heavier weapons will be hardly impeded by something as trivial as a brick wall. However, care must be exercised when using heavy weapons in the urban environment, as they will punch through everything in their path, create secondary fragmentation and generally endanger everyone and everything downrange.

DAMAGE TO THE CITY

Damage to the city may not be desirable, which further restricts the free-fire environment. Seeking to avoid damage to homes,

The urban environment offers a wealth of excellent firing positions and plenty of hard cover. All the traditional rifleman's skills of cover and concealment apply in the city, although some of the applications are novel.

hospitals and holy places is important as these might provide the enemy with propaganda and alienate the local population. Combat can also wreck the infrastructure of a city. Explosions may cut power lines and water pipes, bring down phone cables and sever gas mains, perhaps leading to explosions. The danger of starting fires cannot be

A US sniper waits patiently for a target as comrades conduct a search in Mosul, Iraq, March 2005. Urban terrain is ideal for snipers, who can be invaluable in eliminating a threat without causing collateral damage.

discounted. In a war zone this can be accepted, but some missions, such as peacekeeping or counter-insurgency operations, must avoid this sort of collateral damage.

POPULATIONS AND MOBILITY

Obviously, there is also the problem of population. Non-combatants might not be willing or able to leave the combat area, and might hide hostiles among them. Strict rules of engagement and careful target identification are necessary to avoid a tragedy, though this works in favour of hostiles who will use such restrictions to

their advantage. The problems of distinguishing hostiles from innocent, or even passively hostile, non-combatants have never been completely solved. Mobility is a serious problem in towns – both the lack and ease of it. It can be frustratingly difficult to get to a specific point through a maze of alleyways and streets, which may be well known to local hostiles. Streets may be cluttered by debris and burned-out vehicles, or blocked by seas of rubble where heavy weapons have been used. They might be pitted by craters or packed with refugees.

Hearts and Minds, British Army style. The optical sight of a rifle makes an unlikely toy to impress an Iraqi child with, but the important thing is to build trust through friendly contact. The means are less important than the results.

THREE-BLOCK WAR

Perhaps the worst aspect of urban operations is the need to conduct a 'three-block war'. That is to say, troops may be engaging snipers or dealing with a mortar team that is shelling their base, while trying to protect engineers who are reconnecting the power cables, preventing pilferage from aid supplies and trying to win the support of the population by running a clinic and teaching basic medicine to the locals. They may be doing all of these things in a town where some people want to fight them, some want to steal from them and most want to get on with their lives as best they can, and all of this may be taking place within the space of three city blocks.

This is the nature of urban combat. It is a far cry from the 'gentleman's war' in the North African desert where there were two clearly identified sides. Yet this is what modern troops have to deal with and, with increasing urbanization, it is only going to get worse.

URBAN TERRAIN COMBAT OPERATIONS

The main tools in urban operations are patrols and building clearance. Patrolling may be aggressive in a war zone, with soldiers seeking to locate the enemy and defeat him, or it may take place in a peacekeeping context, but the principle is the same. The use of

PEACEKEEPING ENVIRONMENTS

In a peacekeeping environment the problem might be that there is normal traffic on the roads and people going about their business around the troops. Since the purpose of peacekeeping and counter-insurgency is to allow this sort of activity to go on unhindered, military operations cannot interfere too much with normal life and must work around the normal bustle of town. Getting to the office in the rush hour can be frustrating; conducting an anti-insurgent sweep in the same environment can turn deadly.

On the other hand, cities offer many routes to move around, many of them undercover. In addition to moving along the streets it is possible to use underground rail tunnels, sewers and similar structures to get from point to point unseen. This is especially effective if the enemy does not know of their existence or where the entrances are. Troops who think they have established a secure area can be surprised from within, and enemies who have been bottled up can be secretly resupplied or reinforced, or might melt away through the sewers.

It is also possible to move around above ground, for example by entering a row of houses and breaking through the interior walls to move along the terrace. This is a slow process but can offer a concealed route into a good firing position.

vehicles (for transport and in combat) is problematical. Vehicles are hemmed in by the structure of a city, and are forced to stick to predictable routes. Ambushes are extremely easy to set up in this environment and can be conducted at extremely short range. It is not uncommon to block streets behind a convoy before attacking it in order to prevent escape or assistance. Such obstructions must be cleared quickly to restore mobility.

Armoured vehicles are very vulnerable in urban terrain, but their firepower makes them useful. This means that they must be protected by deployed infantry, who can keep anti-tank teams at a distance while the vehicle-mounted heavy weapons supply fire support when needed; and the

threat of an advancing tank or other armoured vehicle may drive hostiles from their positions.

Troops on the ground need to be able to move in such a way that they can make use of available cover without losing contact with one another, and they must be capable of mutual support. In Northern Ireland it became standard practice for British soldiers to take cover whenever the patrol halted for any reason. It may seem incongruous for a military force to be seen hiding behind gateposts and postboxes on the streets of a British city, but the necessity was discovered in hard-won lessons.

A patrol is fairly visible and may be ambushed or come under sniper fire, in which case response must be both aggressive

and tightly controlled. Troops must not forget the 360-degree combat environment (in three dimensions) while engaging a target to front. Firing positions in the upper storey or roof space of a house can be difficult to locate, and fire may come in from more than one direction, negating the benefits of cover.

Removing an enemy position can be carried out in several ways. In a free-fire area, anti-tank weapons work very well, as do heavy machine-guns or the automatic cannon fitted to many armoured vehicles. Tank guns are also an excellent option. However, where collateral damage must be kept to a minimum, infantry assault is often the only way.

An assault should take the form of leapfrogging rushes from one position of cover to another, covered by the elements that are not moving. Suppressive fire is used to keep the enemy's response to a minimum until the advancing troops can make their final assault.

BUILDING CLEARANCE
At this point, building clearance becomes necessary, unless the enemy can be neutralized by other means such as snipers or by tossing grenades into their position. Urban rooms have one

disadvantage as firing positions: they act as grenade traps. If one comes in, it stays in unless it can be quickly found and thrown back out. Hostiles will then find themselves confined in a small area with a live grenade. If they are lucky, it might be tear gas, which will force a quick exit into the open. A fragmentation grenade in a confined space with hard walls is a deadly prospect.

If the building cannot be cleared by this means, troops have to go in. This is where short, handy 'bullpup' configuration assault rifles or submachine-guns are most useful. Assault shotguns

House clearing technique – in addition to moving down the central corridor, troops can move though internal doors to outflank enemy positions. It is vital to clear each room and not leave hostiles behind the advancing clearance team.

offer some promise for this environment, too.

Clearing a building is a matter of removing hostiles (one way or another) from each room in turn. Suppressive fire must be used with care once friendly troops are in the building. It is common to throw a grenade in through the entry point and follow as soon as it detonates.

Targets must be quickly identified (and distinguished from hostages or non-combatants) and neutralized with overwhelming firepower.

Tactical reloading is vital in building clearance. A soldier confronted with an enemy while his weapon is out of ammunition is in serious trouble. Mutual cover must be given while troops advance, reload and prepare to clear each room in turn. The flimsiness of internal walls must

be remembered. Bullets will go through into adjoining rooms and possibly endanger friendlies, but equally a burst put through a door or wall can eliminate or suppress the enemy long enough to enter the room and make an aimed shot.

Building clearance must be well drilled and coordinated. As well as the possibility of missing targets and being attacked from behind, troops may engage one another or run into traps. Buildings are three-dimensional combat environments where grenades can be dropped down stairwells and hostiles can fire down through holes in the ceiling. Tackling the upper floors can be very dangerous and it is better to eliminate defenders by fire from outside or by inducing them to surrender after taking the ground floor to cut off their escape.

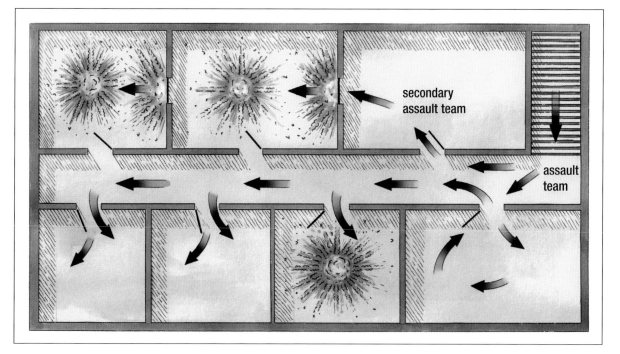

CHAPTER FIVE

SPECIAL FORCES

Virtually every fighting force in history has contained an elite group and/or troops trained and equipped for a specialist role. From the Huscarles who formed the bodyguard of Anglo-Saxon kings, through sharpshooters and rifle-armed troops in the Napoleonic wars to modern hostage-rescue units, there has always been a need for troops who are above the ordinary. These 'Special Forces' may be trained for very unusual combat environments or in skills not needed by ordinary infantrymen. In all cases they are fit, tough, aggressive and highly skilled and, above all, adaptable. Special Forces units often operate without major back-up or support, and must deal with whatever they encounter using only their own resources.

Special Forces units are not only drawn from the military; many nations maintain special police units that share the functions of their military counterparts.

A US Navy SEAL surfaces with his Colt .45 pistol drawn during a combat swimmer training dive May, 2006. The Navy SEALs offer a Special Forces capabilities to the US Navy in every theatre of the world.

MILITARY OPERATIONS

Special Forces units undertake a range of operations that are also carried out by regular soldiers. Their high degree of motivation and training allows them to take these skills to new heights, and sometimes techniques pioneered by Special Forces units become standard throughout the army. In this way, Special Forces units are 'centres of excellence' for military skills as well as sources of advanced training for the regulars.

This does not in any way detract from the function of Special Forces units as elite striking and reconnaissance units. They are very much 'force-multipliers' to modern military

organizations. A small force of experts can get into places that a larger unit would be unable to, at least without being detected, and can cause disruption and dismay to the enemy out of all proportion to their numbers.

To a great extent, the value of Special Forces personnel is not their fighting ability, considerable as it is, but the fact that they can and will take this ability into all environments, appearing, out of the blue, to carry out a mission, then disappearing again before an effective response can be mounted.

Special Forces units are sometimes used to strike at the enemy, for example by destroying

an installation or assassinating a commander. This might be in support of an operation, such as the removal of air-defence radars just before an attack, or may be general harassment, such as the demolition of a bridge to compound the enemy's logistics problems. Reconnaissance is also an important role. For example, one function of the British Special Boat Service is to conduct beach reconnaissance before an amphibious landing.

SPECIAL FORCES INSERTION TECHNIQUES

For a small unit in enemy territory, being spotted means serious trouble. Even if the team breaks contact with the enemy, its mission is likely to be compromised as the enemy will be alerted and perhaps actively searching for the intruders. Under such circumstances it is usually wise to abort the mission and retire to the pick-up point. Therefore, in order to fulfil their function, Special Forces troops must get into the general target area undetected and move to the target without triggering a response. Afterwards, they need to make good their escape.

Remaining undetected can be accomplished in various ways. The closer to their objective that

Combat at night favours the smaller, better trained team over a larger but disorganized body of troops. Special forces train to exploit and even maximise the confusion that darkness causes, using the resulting chaos to cover a disengagement or the completion of the mission.

the team can be inserted, the less chance there will be for accidental discovery. Travelling long distances overland is not usually desirable, though it may allow a very indirect approach to the target.

Insertion may be by any means. Helicopters and various parachuting techniques are often used, as are insertion from water by submarine or boat. In the right conditions, overland insertion is possible, either covertly or by using deception to allay suspicions about the team's vehicle.

AIRBORNE INSERTION

Airborne insertion by helicopter is relatively simple. Whether the helicopters land or the team rappels to ground level on ropes, the noise of the helicopters is itself a drawback. The enemy may not know what has happened in the area, but they will be aware that something has, and may send forces to investigate.

Frequent false helicopter missions may be used as a diversion or deception in the hope that the enemy will tire of chasing around the countryside looking for teams that are not there. However, the risk of losses for nothing more than the creation of a little ambiguity may rule out this prospect.

Helicopter insertion is thus used mainly in remote areas or where the target is extremely localized, such as a hostage situation, rather than being part of a military network. Parachute insertion offers more possibilities for getting Special Forces personnel

US Marine Recon soldiers practice disembarking from a hovering helicopter. Insertion is always dangerous, so the faster it can be accomplished, the better.

into enemy-held territory. Fixed-wing aircraft are faster than helicopters and thus less vulnerable to being intercepted. They also have a longer range, though inserting a team very deep in enemy territory is unusual. Getting back out will be problematical. Parachutes are silent, though very vulnerable if they are spotted while still airborne.

The standard parachute technique that has been in use for many years is the static-line jump. Essentially, the soldier's parachute is fastened to a rail in the aircraft by a cord, which tears a breakaway section off his parachute pack and automatically opens it. This is accompanied by a tremendous jerk, but it does allow insertions at quite low level. In World War II, troops were

It takes a certain kind of person to jump out of an aircraft, especially at high altitude as this special forces soldier is doing. He is undertaking a High Altitude Low Opening (HALO) or Military Free Fall (MFF) insertion.

able to jump from as low as 50m (163ft) in training, and successfully jumped from 76m (250ft) in combat.

Modern static-line jumps are usually from rather higher up than this, partially as a result of changes in parachute design. This is satisfactory when delivering a large combat force that can cope with the inevitable scatter due to wind and aircraft movement during the drop, but for a small

team it may not be acceptable. There is also the risk of detection and being shot down.

AVOIDING DETECTION

There are two solutions to the problem of detection: fly extremely low or extremely high. The former offers a good chance of remaining undetected and the latter places the aircraft beyond the range of most ground-based weapons. When jumping from a high-flying aircraft, Special Forces troops cannot use conventional High Altitude High Opening (HAHO) techniques as this would leave them dangling from a parachute for long periods. Even the most manoeuvrable chute would likely

be blown well off course by any significant wind, hopelessly scattering the team.

High Altitude Low Opening (HALO) or Military Free Fall (MFF) delivery is used instead. Essentially, the Special Forces soldiers leave the aircraft and simply allow themselves to fall until they reach low altitude. Canopy (parachute) deployment can be manually or altimeter controlled. The altimeter will deploy the canopy at a preset altitude; though the soldier can choose to open his parachute sooner.

Oxygen supplies are usually needed for HALO jumps, to avoid altitude sickness when jumping

EARLY SPECIAL FORCES

The forerunners of the SAS were the Long-Range Desert Group, which made a nuisance of itself in North Africa during World War II using light vehicles (jeeps) to carry a heavy armament of machine-guns. Avoiding heavy combat, the jeep-mounted force could penetrate into the enemy rear, where security was relatively lax, and attack vulnerable targets such as airfields and supply dumps before vanishing under cover of darkness.

Other Special Forces units created in World War II included the German 'Brandenburgers', who were intended to cause chaos in support of an attack by penetrating the Allied rear area dressed as Allied troops and engaging in sabotage, ambush and misdirection. This tactic was used during the invasion of Norway in 1940 and the Ardennes Offensive in 1944. Success was limited, though some moderately useful results were obtained.

from a very high-flying aircraft. Special clothing is needed to cope with the extreme cold at altitude. Experiments with HALO delivery of equipment have been successful, and Special Forces units can be resupplied or supported by the same methods used for their insertion, though accuracy of delivery is a factor.

The alternative, Low Altitude Low Opening (LALO), has been the subject of extensive experimentation. US troops assaulting Corregidor during World War II were delivered from very low altitude to ensure accuracy – the only suitable landing area was a golf course. A high proportion of jump casualties was considered acceptable for this operation, though not when inserting a small team.

In combined operations with the US Navy, Albanian Special Forces soldiers fast rope from a US Navy MH-60S Nighthawk helicopter, assigned to Helicopter Sea Combat Squadron Two Six (HSC-26), Detachment Two, during Exercise Adriatic Engagement 2005.

Modern LALO techniques use a static line and are quite sophisticated, allowing accurate delivery of troops with minimal casualties. Variants include tree-jumping, a technique of jumping into thick forest or jungle and hoping that the parachute snags on a branch. The soldier then climbs down a rope attached to his parachute harness. However, this technique is not suitable for Special Forces operations because it tends to cause many casualties, who then need to be rescued by helicopter, with all the problems associated with helicopter insertion.

INSERTION IN WATER

Another, more feasible, system is to deliver parachutists from very

BEACH RECONNAISSANCE

A story related by an ex-Paratrooper tells of an encounter with a Special Boat Service beach-reconnaissance operation. The Paratroopers were to go ashore in the Falklands from landing craft, a new experience for them. Plans were made and dates shifted, and the assault went in a little earlier than expected.

As the Paratroopers charged up the beach towards less open territory, they spotted what they thought was an enemy solider and tried to subdue him. Their intended prisoner was having none of it and fought off several Paratroopers before they realized he was shouting abuse at them in English. The resulting discussion was a little acrimonious but revealed that the intruder was actually an SBS man reconnoitring for their landing, which was scheduled for the next day.

He then added casually: 'So, how did you get through the minefield?'

A Greek Police Special Forces unit disembarks from a small boat. Many police forces maintain specialist units for hostage-rescue and counter-terrorist work.

low level into water. Flying extremely low, the delivery aircraft pulls up almost vertical, with the tailgate open, and the troops more or less fall out. A static-line chute briefly deploys, slowing them enough to survive hitting the water, and the team then swims ashore.

More conventional waterborne insertion methods involve the team going ashore in small boats from a surface vessel or submarine. Some submarines have been specially converted to deliver small units close to the shore. Ironically, modern nuclear attack boats are not the best-suited platforms for this role; conventional, diesel-electric subs tend to be better. However, all the submarine needs to do is get the team within striking distance of the shore. From there, they can proceed under their own power.

However the team is inserted, care must be taken to ensure that no obvious traces are left.

Parachutes, boats and other objects that cannot be taken with the team must be hidden, and all traces of the landing eliminated before the team can move off.

INFILTRATION, EXFILTRATION AND EVASION

It is no surprise, given the importance of being able to move stealthily, that one of the most important parts of the SAS selection process is Escape-and-Evasion exercises. These test the soldier and his skills to the limit and are one of the hardest parts of his training.

When moving to and from the target area, the Special Forces team needs to be able to move quickly, avoiding patrols and static guardposts as well as contact with the local population who might give them away. The team must also be careful not to move into hazardous areas such as minefields and bogs. Stealth

and caution must be balanced against the need to reach the target and carry out the mission on schedule.

Assuming that the enemy has not detected the insertion, the Special Forces team has the advantage that, however alert the enemy may be, they are not actively looking for the team. Patrols may be predictable, routine and half-hearted, especially in areas 'known' to be safe.

The Special Forces team may know in advance many of the positions occupied by the enemy, his strength, patrolling habits and so forth. However, intelligence is never perfect and the team must be alert and ready to change its route frequently.

Moving through potentially hostile terrain requires making the best possible use of natural and artificial cover. Some measures are obvious, such as moving below crestlines or along stream

A US Navy SEAL trooper in Afghanistan. When combating insurgents who simply will not come out and fight in the open, Special Forces offer a chance to play them at their own game – and win.

gulleys to avoid being skylined, and these can be applied to man-made cover. Drainage ditches and culverts can be used to move alongside a road; fences and walls provide a barrier to observation in built-up areas.

It is best to detour around manned guardposts, but if these must be passed, then the Special Forces team must make use of all available cover, including shadows and obstructions. It is important to be able to think one's self into the enemy sentry's shoes – what can he see from his position? Is there dead ground or an area of deep shadow that will allow the team to pass by unobserved?

It is possible to cross even quite open areas by using shadows and whatever concealment is available; so long as this soldier does not allow his silhouette to be outlined above the undergrowth his chances are good.

Bad weather is a useful ally. Nobody likes being cold and wet, and guards and sentries are more likely to seek cover rather than carry out their duties diligently. Rain tends to make people hunch up and look down, and this is not conducive to good observation of their surroundings. Rain and wind can mask noise as well.

Brute-force infiltration measures such as eliminating guards, cutting fences and breaking cameras are of limited use. Sooner or later they will be noticed and this will quickly alert the defenders. Such heavy-handed measures should only be used in

the last phase of an approach to the target or in an emergency.

Once the mission has been carried out, the team will need to get away again. This is also true where a mission has been aborted or where soldiers have been captured and have escaped. If possible, a stealthy departure using a different path to the approach is best, but if the enemy is actively searching for the team, then a more hurried evasion will be necessary.

ESCAPE
Escapes from capture are increasingly unlikely the longer the solider has been in enemy hands. The troops who capture a Special Forces solider are unlikely to be experienced at handling prisoners and may make mistakes that allow for an escape. But as a prisoner is

processed and passed to the rear, his chances diminish rapidly due to increased distance form friendly territory, tiredness and perhaps ill-treatment, and the difficulty of maintaining his bearings as he is transported.

Whether escaping capture or breaking contact with the enemy, escape is very much a matter of making use of time and distance. The enemy will have a rough idea of how far the soldier or team can have gone in the time since last contact, and will have to search this area. Blindly charging in the direction of an extraction or rendezvous point will play into the hands of the pursuers of course, so the team must take an evasive route. This will slow them down but offers a better chance of escape. The assumption is that the team will depart the area of last contact with the enemy as rapidly as possible, and as a rule this will be true. However, there have been cases of escaped prisoners of war cheekily remaining just outside the detention facility for days or even weeks until the search had moved on or been given up. This is an extremely risky option but if successful it allows a clean break with pursuit.

More normally, the team will move as quickly as possible towards friendly territory or a suitable extraction point, making use of cover and terrain as far as possible. It is likely that the enemy will patrol roads and place roadblocks on bridges and other obvious routes, so these must be avoided.

PROFESSIONAL RIVALRY

The Royal Marines and the Parachute Regiment both vie for the crown of Britain's elite soldiers, and personnel will often do one another down or even fight over their rivalry – when they are not fighting shoulder-to-shoulder against the nation's enemies.

There are good and deep reasons for this kind of clash between elites in peacetime. It is a product of the group narcissism and elitist attitudes that are necessary to forge an excellent combat force. To be the best, soldiers must believe that they are indeed better than everyone else, and admitting that a rival formation may be almost as good comes hard.

But ask a Para or Marine why he dislikes his counterparts and he will not tell you about the rivalry, or the remote possibility that they may be a contender for his unit's laurels. He is more likely to shrug and inform you that 'they wear the wrong colour hats'.

Special Forces personnel are trained to avoid detection and evade pursuit. They are also trained to resist interrogation, but the best way to do that is not to get caught. Continual escape and evasion exercises like this one keep skills honed to a fine edge.

Tracking dogs are difficult to evade, but it can be done. By laying a confusing trail or crossing water, evading soldiers hope to make the dogs lose the scent or double back on themselves. Killing dogs is a last-resort option.

Navigation is important in evasion. It is easy to get lost and move further into danger rather than away from it. Moving at night aids concealment but increases the risk of accidents and becoming lost. Direct movement is dangerous; it is far better to move from cover to cover, lying up for as long as necessary before attempting the next move.

TRACKED BY DOGS

Despite all the modern electronic sensors available to military forces, dogs remain one of the most serious threats to evading Special Forces personnel. Hiding from visual observation does no good if the pursuers are able to track by scent. The best way to avoid this is to lay a confusing trail, doubling back around obstructions and across clear areas in the hope that the dogs will lose the scent.

Running water is excellent for obscuring a scent trail, but it is not enough just to cross a river or stream and hope for the best. If the pursuers can find the point where the water was left, they can pick up the scent again. It is best to enter the water and move along the stream for some distance before leaving, ideally on hard ground where there will be little sign to follow. By breaking the scent and physical/visual trails at the same point, it is possible to evade even tracker dogs.

A successful evasion requires reaching a place of safety. This may mean a rendezvous/pick -up point or friendly forces, or possibly crossing a border into friendly territory. There is always a hazard from one's own side, so approaches to friendly or neutral forces must be made carefully. Special Forces soldiers are taught that the escape is not complete until they reach a friendly base. Relaxing a moment too soon may lead to disaster if the rendezvous point has been compromised or enemy forces are closer than the team supposed.

SNIPING

Snipers are not always considered 'Special Forces' as such, but they share many common traits. Snipers, however, are more specialized. Their skills focus on stealth, observation and marksmanship.

Snipers usually operate with a 'spotter' who shares many of their skills. The spotter helps locate the target, protects the sniper by keeping up all-round observation while the sniper is setting up a shot, and sometimes relays reconnaissance data or requests for support back to base. The spotter also observes the results of a shot and the enemy's reactions to it.

A single sniper can play havoc with the enemy. He can shoot a general or other important figure, disrupting command and control functions, or render an enemy force impotent with a few shots. A combat patrol that loses its leader, communications man and the first soldier to show any initiative thereafter may be driven under cover and remain there for hours after the sniper has moved on. If this keeps happening an enemy force can be severely disrupted.

Snipers can also attack objects. In World War I, some snipers were issued armour-piercing ammunition to shoot out the breechblocks of enemy machine-guns. Another soldier could quickly replace a gunner but a smashed gun was out of combat for much longer. The same principle extends to communications equipment, radar sets and other expensive and complex devices.

In addition to the obvious effects of a bullet out of nowhere,

snipers can be invaluable in observing the enemy and reporting on his dispositions. They can also call in artillery or air support. On one occasion during the Vietnam War, a sniper and his spotter were able to pin a large enemy force with a few accurate shots and then call in a flight of aircraft to drop napalm on them, inflicting huge casualties and escaping scot-free.

A sniper's main weapon is his rifle, and although many modern battlefield rifles are capable of accurate, long-range fire, a sniping weapon is a precision instrument above the level of common 'battle'

rifles. Until recently, sniper weapons were usually produced in standard calibres similar to rifles and machine-guns used by infantry. Today, specialist heavy sniping weapons are available in .50 calibre and even 25mm (1in). These large weapons are capable of firing a bullet over very long distances, and their ammunition

A French Foreign Legion sniper team in Sarajevo, 1996. The high vantage point gives a good field of fire and – sometimes more importantly – observation while making detection unlikely. Other soldiers remain out of sight but assist the sniper as extra eyes as well as security for his back.

is less prone to wind effects than smaller, lighter rounds.

Sniping rifles have long, heavy barrels that increase their accuracy, and advanced sights graduated out to ranges far beyond the distance where most soldiers can hit anything. They require special ammunition of extremely high and consistent quality for optimum results. Some sniper rifles, for example, the

A British sniper team camouflaged in 'ghillie suits' lie in wait. The sniper is armed with an Accuracy International L96 rifle while his spotter uses binoculars to find a target and to observe the results of the shot.

Walther WA 2000, are incredibly accurate but too fragile for field use. These weapons are excellent for 'law-enforcement' or hostage-rescue situations but need too much careful handling to survive in the field.

Military sniper weapons tend to be robust and capable of retaining their accuracy in a harsh environment. One example is the Galil Sniper, developed from the excellent Galil assault rifle. It is by no means an exceptionally accurate rifle as sniper weapons go, but its toughness allows it to retain its accuracy in conditions that may defeat other weapons.

SNIPER POSITIONS

Snipers shoot using positions that look odd to observers but offer the most stable firing position possible. The most important thing is to keep the weapon still and avoid movement during the shot – which means from the final seconds of aim through to the instant the bullet leaves the barrel.

Where possible, a solid object is used as a rest for the rifle. Many weapons include a bipod or monopod, which is useful when prone or firing over a rest, but snipers are trained to create a stable firing platform with their body where necessary. Often the

weapon is supported in a cradle made by the user's non-trigger hand, which cups the bottom of the stock and rests, in turn, in the crook of the trigger hand's elbow.

It is vital that the user's cheek always rests in exactly the same position on the weapon, his eye the same distance from the sight on each shot. He must relax to avoid muscle tremors and hold his breath as he takes up the final aim and pulls the trigger. By keeping as much of the biomechanics of his firing position the same as is humanly possible, the sniper eliminates variation from the shot – in other words, he ensures that the bullet will go where he wants it to.

The sniper is unlikely to be able to aim directly at the target unless it stays still for a while at a fairly short range and there is no wind. More likely he will have to aim-off to compensate for wind and bullet drop due to gravity, and may have to 'lead' a moving target so that bullet and target reach a common point at the same time. The sniper who is about to shoot thus selects what appears to be a spot of empty air and aims his rifle at it, ceasing even to breathe. He touches the trigger and the shot is made. Snipers have made confirmed kills at 1800m (5905ft) and at shorter but impressive ranges, even in windy conditions. To those near the target, seeing a man drop and having no idea where the shot came from is a terrifying experience.

Successful sniping is, of course, more than marksmanship. The sniper must be able to get into a

firing position and remain there long enough to make his shot. He must also escape afterwards. Snipers are thus masters of camouflage and the observation skills they need to make their camouflage truly effective. They may take hours to crawl a short distance, since the human eye picks up movement more readily than a static object. Sniping is thus an exercise in patience.

A sniper may have to escape after his shot. If he is firing in support of other troops, this is not normally necessary, but where he has infiltrated close to an enemy position, he will need either to

sneak away amid a search or escape in a quicker manner. Selecting a firing position with access to good cover for the initial escape is a vital skill for the sniper who plans to collect his pension some day.

The last (bottom right) sight picture in each group represents an aim point directly over the target. To compensate for target movement, wind and bullet drop, aim-off is necessary. Some scopes are marked with aim-off points graduated for different ranges, but hitting a target even with a sophisticated sight to help requires great skill.

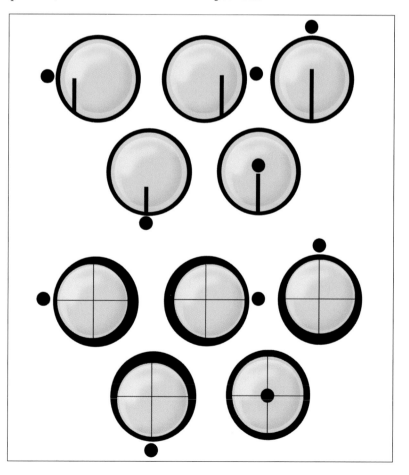

CLOSE-PROTECTION METHODS

Special police and military close-protection units exist to ensure the safety of government ministers and other VIPs. These units sometimes operate overtly, but ostentatiously surrounding oneself with 'minders' is more commonly associated with celebrities whose possession of bodyguards is part of their public image.

Uniformed (and usually armed) personnel are often assigned to deter attack on VIPs, but these are not usually Special Forces operatives. The latter are more likely to be unobtrusive, blending in with the plethora of aides, drivers, waiters and other support personnel around the VIP. This not only prevents a hostile force from easily identifying the

bodyguards and eliminating them at the outset of an attack but also allows covert observation of the surroundings on the part of the close protection team.

The purpose of close-protection units is not to eliminate threats to the principal but to ensure his safety. In the midst of a crisis these may seem to be the same thing, but in fact there are critical differences in approach. A close-protection team needs to exchange fire with attackers, eliminating whatever targets it can as quickly and efficiently as possible, but suppressing the hostiles long enough to get the principal to safety is more important. A team that forgets its primary mission to engage in a gun battle will likely fail to carry out its mission.

US Army Gen John Abizaid, Central Command (CENTCOM) commander of all theatre operations in Iraq, is escorted to Polish Maj Gen Mieczyslaw Bieniek's office for a briefing at Camp Babylon, Iraq, March 2004.

OBSERVATION AND INTERCEPTION

The primary tool of close protection units is observation. The sooner a threat is identified, the greater the chance of dealing with it successfully. Ideally, most avenues of attack are closed off by good preparation work, denying the 'bad guys' the opportunity they need to make an effective attack. If prevention fails, early identification of the threat can allow the close-protection team time to react or force the hostiles to make a low-percentage, possibly disrupted, attack rather than a well-coordinated one carried out on their own terms.

This is especially important when dealing with the possibility of suicide bombers. Someone who has already chosen to die for his cause will not be deterred by the possibility of being shot by a bodyguard as he triggers his bomb. However, nobody is prepared to die to fail. If it looks likely that the bomber will be eliminated long before he gets within striking range, he is likely to wait for a better opportunity or a softer target.

If pre-emption or interception fails, then the close-protection team will have to react to events as they happen. It is vital that they be positioned to do so. Usually, there will be a bodyguard who represents the last line of defence and a team of other operatives positioned to interfere with any attempt to approach to shoot at the principal. Formations must be fluid and well drilled; a protection team cannot simply form a tight phalanx around the VIP and hope for the best.

MOBILE PROTECTION

Protection is difficult when on the move, and a well-drilled team is vital here. Each man must be able to manoeuvre to cover his sector, leaving no angle unobserved, and must change positions to deal with circumstances as they arise. If the team is to walk past the mouth of an alley, someone needs to move a little ahead to ensure that it is not filled with wild-eyed assassins.

If an area ahead offers a visual obstruction, a member of the team needs to move away from the group so that he can see or shoot into it.

This is equally the case when travelling in vehicles. An escort vehicle needs to be able to check out suspect cars that want to pass, or block an intersection so that the principal's vehicle and the escorts can remain together. Fixed distances should not be maintained; terrorists have been known to use the lead escort car to time a roadside bomb, having observed the routine and precision of the bodyguard team.

Entering and leaving vehicles and buildings are also times of danger that require good drills and flexibility. Members of the close-protection team need to ensure that the vehicle or building is safe before the principal enters, and to provide all-round observation as he enters or leaves. It is easy to fixate on a particular task, such as watching the far side of the road, and not notice that another member of the team has been moved out of position by circumstances such as traffic or passing pedestrians. The team needs to remain fluid and cover all angles in a rapidly changing situation.

Routines and fixed positions must be avoided, and this is an essential part of close-protection training. A team that is predictable is a team that is ineffective. There will always be gaps in any protection set-up, but if they are fleeting and random then the risk is minimal. On the other hand, predictability makes such gaps deadly.

Security personnel provide all-round observation and protection for General Norman Schwarzkopf as he arrives in Kuwait. A good close protection team will reduce the odds of attack as far as possible and be able to respond flexibly.

UNDER ATTACK

If all else fails, then the job of the close-protection squad is to get the principal to safety as a fast as possible, though without rushing headlong into other dangers. Marksmanship, weapon handling and the ability to disable opponents quickly at close quarters are vital if an attack has to be

A simulated hostage-rescue operation during a training exercise. The state of the hostages can alter the mission parameters greatly. These victims cannot run to safety under their own power while the rescuers engage the terrorists – but neither can they blunder into a line of fire.

stopped by force, but teamwork is equally important. An attack may be a diversion, so some members of the team must continue to cover other angles. Knowing who will provide body cover, who will return fire and who will open the car door to get the VIP inside is vital – there will be no time to correct mistakes.

Close protection requires a good deal of intelligence and adaptability in personnel, along with excellent teamwork and the ability to remain alert during long periods of mundane activity. Fighting skills are important but come second to these factors; a team that prevents an attack has

done the job just as well as one that bags several 'bad guys' – perhaps better.

HOSTAGE RESCUE TECHNIQUES

Despite the best security measures that can be implemented, terrorists and criminals do sometimes take hostages. Whether for political ends, in the hope of obtaining ransom money or out of desperation, the end result is the same. If the hostage-takers cannot be persuaded to free their captives and surrender, then rescue becomes necessary.

Military hostage-rescue operations are not subtle. By the time matters have reached the stage

Hostage-takers will generally try to render their victims as helpless as possible by physical measures. The longer someone spends as a hostage, the more mentally and psychologically helpless they tend to become. Trained personnel tend to retain their will to escape longer than civilians.

how they are armed and where they are located. This helps in the planning before the operation and in distinguishing the hostages from hostage-takers in the midst of the assault.

when Special Forces must enter a building or aircraft to get someone out, the gloves are well and truly off. Special Forces troops know that they face determined opponents who are ready and able to use lethal force against the hostages or rescuers. They must go in hard and fast, and not give the 'bad guys' a chance to react. The faster the rescue is over, the better the chances for the hostages.

This does involve an element of risk for the hostages. Special Forces teams must make split-second shoot/no-shoot decisions in a very confused situation. Even the most highly skilled personnel do make mistakes, and bullets do miss their intended target. However, rescue units are not committed until the situation is very grave indeed. It is highly unlikely that hostages would be better off if no rescue was attempted, whatever the odds.

INTELLIGENCE GATHERING

Before an assault is made, all available information is gathered.

In a lengthy siege, this can be very elaborate, involving hidden cameras and microphones as well as more mundane sources of information such as released hostages, witnesses and plans of the target obtained from local authorities.

The hostage-rescue unit ideally needs to know how many hostiles there are, what they look like,

GAINING ENTRY

The most critical phase of a rescue operation is to gain entry to wherever the hostages are being held. This is especially difficult in the case of an aircraft or other vehicle that is parked in the open. Deception and distraction can be used to allow the team to get as close as possible before the assault is launched, but if the

US Air Force personnel plot strategies prior to making a hostage rescue attempt during tactical training at Langley Air Force Base, Virginia.

An SAS team engaged in room-clearance. Each man covers his sector and trusts his team mates to do the same. Second-guessing one another or leaving an area uncovered can be fatal for the team and for the people they are trying to rescue, so training as a team is as important as individual skills.

through walls and ceilings using frame charges. This allows the Special Forces soldiers to appear suddenly in unexpected – and, hopefully, unguarded – places. Even if the hostage-takers are expecting an assault, they are more likely to be watching doors and windows than walls, and this, coupled with the shock of being attacked, may lead to fatal hesitation.

THE ASSAULT

Once inside the target, the assault team must move fast and eliminate its targets quickly. Short, controlled bursts of automatic fire are a favourite technique to disable hostiles rapidly, and weapons fire must obviously be tightly controlled to avoid endangering team-mates and hostages.

Room-clearance is drilled to a fine art by hostage-rescue teams. Each man has a sector to cover and must trust his team-mates to clear their sector or cover hallways outside. He must do his own job without becoming distracted. Whether a stun grenade, tear gas or some other distraction has gone into the room first, personnel entering a room occupied by armed hostiles face severe danger. Their safety is best guaranteed by extreme aggression and total ruthlessness.

This aggression manifests itself in a fast-moving assault. Doors are kicked in or shot off their hinges, and walls are sometimes blasted through. Stun grenades are thrown round corners or through doorways and followed by personnel with every intention of killing anyone

hostage-takers become aware of what is going on, there is a risk that they will panic or perhaps deliberately begin killing the hostages. In this case the assault will have to go in from wherever personnel are located.

Tear gas and smoke grenades are sometimes useful to cover an assault, though both can take a few seconds to become effective, which may be counterproductive. Surprise is the best weapon the rescue team has at its disposal, and this is gained by a sudden attack accompanied by noise and confusion.

A good entry usually means a successful operation. The team will usually enter at several points. Ideally, hostiles near these points will be eliminated by snipers or by the first man into the target. Stun grenades, which make a lot of light and noise, and disorient anyone nearby, can gain a Special Forces team a vital second to enter, identify the target and eliminate hostiles before they can harm the hostages or attack the rescue team.

Hostage-rescue units can enter via the obvious doors and windows, but may also blast

they find armed on the other side. The purpose of the assault is not, however, to kill the hostage-takers. This is simply something that must be done. The aim of the operation is to rescue the hostages, and eliminating their captors is a necessary task along the way to achieving this. Behind the clearance teams, Special Forces soldiers will usher the hostages to safety, possibly escorting or guiding them out through smoke or tear gas. Other team members will search for concealed hostiles and other hazards such as booby-traps in the wake of the assault team.

A 'bad guy' who throws down his weapon may well be shot anyway – if things have reached the point where an assault is necessary, then there is no margin for error and the clearance team

A stun grenade. These devices create a very bright light and tremendous noise but are unlikely to seriously harm anyone. They are used to distract hostiles or make them 'freeze' for a moment while Special Forces troops make their assault.

might not realize the terrorist is surrendering in time to make a no-shoot decision.

Where possible, prisoners will be taken, though in the chaos of an assault there is not time for the repeated warnings and relatively gentle arrest procedures of police officers. The hostage-takers have made it necessary for the authorities to send troops in to rescue the captives – they can hardly expect the rescue team to risk their own safety and that of the innocent hostages in order to give a terrorist the benefit of the doubt.

SPECIAL SITUATIONS

Rescues involving trains, aircraft, buses, etc are especially problematical. It is sometimes possible to eliminate the hostage-takers by using snipers, but more often the vehicle has to be entered and the hostiles taken out at close quarters. Getting close enough to do so may require stopping the vehicle. Ground vehicles and trains can be stopped by obstructing their path or deflating tyres; aircraft will have to land to refuel and can usually be kept on the ground once they are down.

Once the situation is contained and the hostage-takers are unable to move their vehicle, they may become sufficiently demoralized

Italian Air Force troops practising personnel recovery from a vehicle-borne hostage situation. Everyone knows his job – some troopers extract the captives while others deal with the terrorists.

to surrender. If not, an assault will be necessary. Gaining access to a large vehicle, particularly an aircraft, is problematical due to the height involved. All means of entry will be used, such as emergency and maintenance access ways in the case of aircraft and trains.

Sometimes it is possible to approach the target vehicle by stealth or deception. Rescue units have approached aircraft by pretending to be flight engineers

Building assault should be carried out using as many entry points as possible. The trooper goes in with his weapon ready, and anyone armed nearby is a target. Once his immediate surroundings are secure he can begin moving on to his objectives.

coming to refuel the aircraft or by bringing food or other supplies demanded by the hostage-takers. Distractions are used whenever possible. These range from the relatively straightforward, such as detonating stun grenades against the hull of the vehicle, to inventive measures such as noisy jet or helicopter activity nearby.

As with buildings, once entry is gained, the rescue team needs to proceed quickly through the vehicle and eliminate any hostiles encountered with precise and overwhelming firepower.

Clearing a long vehicle such as a train or aircraft is less complex in some ways than clearing a building, but very difficult in others. There is usually only one route and there may be a lot of

innocents along any line of fire. The key to all hostage rescues is to gain as much information as possible, plan well, then go in hard and fast using distraction and deception wherever possible.

COUNTER-INSURGENCY TECHNIQUES

One key role for Special Forces is in defeating insurgency and returning rebellious areas to government control. Experience has shown that while large conventional forces can sometimes succeed in bringing an insurgency under control, units trained and equipped for large-scale conventional warfare can be too clumsy to deal effectively with guerrillas, especially where they enjoy considerable local support.

There are several problems when attempting to deal with an insurgency. The insurgents themselves are usually 'home-grown', i.e. they are part of the local society, whereas the forces opposing them are not. The local population has been described as a 'sea' in which the 'fish' (the insurgents) swim. Guerrillas and terrorists can move unseen among the general populace, gathering intelligence and making their preparations, until they are ready to strike. Afterwards, they can melt back into the background and disappear.

Obtaining information about the insurgents can be very difficult. It is possible that many locals share their grievances, even if they do not actively support the insurgency, and there is often a reluctance to talk to the authorities in such cases. The

insurgents know the population and may enforce silence through various means.

Some insurgent groups have been known to act as an unofficial police force, punishing criminals and thus gaining the support of the populace. Others use the threat of violence to maintain secrecy. Most groups do a little of both, and try to portray themselves as acting on behalf of the general public.

Penetrating this culture to gain information can be very difficult. The populace have to be convinced that it is in their interest to talk to the authorities, and that they will not come to harm by doing so. On a large scale, this may be done using propaganda aimed at discrediting the insurgents or showing them in a bad light, while demonstrating the benefits the authorities bring. Special Forces units can take a more personal approach, however, working closely with the locals to win their respect and trust. This is part of a 'hearts and minds' approach.

The other main problem in dealing with insurgency is that the insurgents know the local terrain, having lived there for many years. They can move easily through areas that outsiders may get lost in, or find impenetrable, and can obtain supplies and support wherever the public are either sympathetic or frightened into complicity.

US Navy personnel aboard a MH-60S Nighthawk helicopter practise suppressing fire using an M240G machine gun, during urban assault training with USN SEALs at Fort Knox.

Large-scale military forces cannot act in this way, and are often seen as blindly blundering around the countryside or tied to their bases and strong points.

While patrolling the roads and guarding the towns are part of counter-insurgency work, it has been shown again and again that more is needed. The missing factor is the ability to get in among the populace to gain information and to fight the insurgents on their own terms. If the insurgents can strike,

Special Forces personnel are often called upon to carry everything they will need with them while on a patrol or mission. A high standard of fitness is required if soldiers are to move and fight under a heavy load.

then hide among the populace, the authorities need to get the locals to tell them where the guerrillas are. If they melt into the jungle, the authorities need to go into the jungle to find them.

Armoured vehicles and air support have their part to play but for truly effective counter-insurgency warfare the tool of choice is the Special Forces team, which can meet the insurgent on his own terms, and defeat him. Special Forces teams are often very small – four-man units are common – but well equipped. Where the bulk of a nation's

armed forces will have standard equipment, often of basic quality, Special Forces units are sometimes allowed to pick their own equipment or obtain it privately, and will be armed with the best weapons available. These small teams may have to operate without support for long periods, sometimes in quite hostile terrain, and are very self-reliant.

In such small units, there is a necessity for each man to be able to perform several different roles, though usually each will have a specialist area such as demolitions, medical aid, marks-manship and so forth in addition to his generally very high level of abilities as a soldier. In the counter-insurgency role, Special Forces units may conduct a strike or become involved in combat with enemy forces, but this is not

RECONNAISSANCE AND INTELLIGENCE GATHERING

One vital role for Special Forces troops in the counter-insurgency role is to gather information on the enemy's numbers, whereabouts, armament and intentions. This can be done by direct infiltration in some cases, but is more often accomplished by covert observation and reconnaissance.

A Special Forces unit can gather a wealth of information about the enemy by moving into his territory and quietly observing what he does. This may go entirely unnoticed, especially if the insurgents' attention is on the activities of large-scale conventional forces. There is an expectation that a power that has large high-technology forces available will not 'get personal' in the way that

deep penetration patrols by small units tend to be. If the enemy is unaware of the presence of Special Forces units and has no reason to suspect they are active in his territory, their work will be so much easier.

Intelligence gathering can take the form of simply observing movements of personnel and vehicles through an area. What may seem like innocent civilian activity at first glance may be revealed as something more sinister by careful observation, and this information can be used to plan an attack or call in air or artillery support on the unsuspecting enemy.

Observation is made easier by night-vision equipment and other technological

aids, but in the end it is the capabilities of the soldiers involved that count most. The ability to pick up on subtle clues, to track the movements of hostile forces, and the capability to remain undetected while doing it are worth more than any electronic device.

Intelligence can also be gathered by talking to people. Establishing communications with the locals obviously requires being able to speak a language they understand, and many Special Forces personnel are at least passable speakers of one or more foreign languages. It is also necessary to convince the locals that they want to talk to the Special Forces personnel, of course. How units relate to local people is discussed below.

their primary role. If possible, they will avoid contact with enemy forces and concentrate on getting the job done without becoming entangled in combat against superior numbers.

PRISONER INTERROGATION

Another way to discover information about the enemy is to ask his personnel. Naturally, few combatants – regulars, irregulars and terrorists alike – will volunteer information to the enemy without being induced to do so in some way.

Torture of prisoners is forbidden by various conventions, and Special Forces personnel are more likely to face this kind of treatment if captured than to mete it out. Special Forces

training includes techniques to help the soldier withstand interrogation, though of course the best way of all is to avoid capture. For this reason, Escape-and-Evasion techniques are an important part of the Special Forces' training curriculum.

Without beating information out of a captured enemy combatant, it is still possible to obtain a wealth of information from him by the use of good interrogation techniques. These make use of a range of human emotions and characteristics. Any captured personnel will quite naturally fear for their safety and be in at least a nervous condition. This can be exploited in many cases, with captured personnel offering

Many armed forces train interpreters to assist their troops in interrogation techniques and also simply talking to the locals. Here US troops are questioning a villager during a counter-insurgency sweep.

information in the hope of securing their own personal safety (whether or not it is actually under threat).

Effective interrogation requires captured personnel to be isolated from the moral support of their comrades and deprived of their status within the group. This is useful for several reasons. If the captured hostile can be convinced that his comrades have 'spilled their guts' in return for favours, food or even release, he may feel that it is not worth holding out.

Friendly contact with the locals is vital to counter-insurgency operations. Here a US soldier greets local Afghan children during his patrol aboard a small All Terrain Vehicle (ATV). In the end it is the support of the people that dictates whether an insurgency thrives or withers.

Information can be cross-referenced to verify it – with no chance to agree on a common story, lies will be readily apparent. Isolation will intensify the enemy's nervousness and unease, and the very natural desire for acceptance and status within a group may lead him to seek favour with his captors. The only currency he has to trade for this is information. He will thus tend to cooperate with whichever of his captors seems the most likely to react favourably. This is the classic 'good cop/bad cop' set-up where one interrogator is harsh and another more sympathetic towards the captive.

HEARTS AND MINDS

Defeating an insurgency is somewhat different to fighting a conventional war. For one thing, targets are less clearly defined – there is no sharp us/them divide. Generally, a country can be persuaded to cease hostilities once the conflict turns against it, and once a treaty has been agreed, it will be enforced by the signing nations on their own armed forces.

An insurgency is usually the result of a segment of the population trying to further its own agenda. There may be no central direction; insurgencies are often decentralized, with several groups vaguely cooperating with,

or opposed to, the authorities for their own reasons. However, even if an insurgency has some central political guidance, a negotiated settlement might be unacceptable. It may also be unenforceable, for example where several splinter groups decide that a settlement is not in their interests, and the majority of the insurgents are unable to convince them to accept it. In this case the only possibility is to find and defeat the insurgents, and it is usually necessary to inflict some defeats upon them to convince them not to negotiate in the first place. The key here is not the guerrillas themselves but the general populace. An insurgency cannot exist where the populace has turned on it. Informed on, denied supplies and freedom of movement, and perhaps even deliberately lured into traps, the insurgents will eventually be either caught or killed, or else be unable to operate.

'Winning hearts and minds' rather than simply fighting the insurgents was the strategy that eventually yielded success in the Malayan Emergency. However much political ideology may be involved in an insurgency, this will not automatically generate popular support. The insurgents will play upon legitimate grievances among the general public and try to create an environment in which the populace sees its interests best served by supporting, or at least not opposing, the guerrillas.

The authorities need to change this attitude, and Special Forces units are a powerful way of effecting such change. A small squad of men is less threatening than a large military presence, and Special Forces units rarely arrive as a military force anyway. Instead, they present themselves as friends and benefactors. An understanding of the local language and culture allows the unit to fit in rather than intruding, and to establish friendly contact. After this, the team can begin helping the locals.

GREATEST IMPACT

Insurgencies tend to have the most support in deprived areas (urban or rural) where life is hard and the authorities are both remote and seemingly uninterested in the fate of the people. It is here that the Special Forces team can have the greatest impact.

The team's medical expert can set up a clinic, treating diseases and injuries and giving advice on health and first aid. He can teach the locals how to improve their quality of life and health in general by basic but effective measures such as hygiene, waste disposal and sanitation. He can also teach skills that will be useful long after the team has moved on, including pre- and ante-natal care, diet and nutrition.

Engineering skills can be used to help the locals build homes and other structures, ranging from irrigation ditches to small bridges. Where possible, locally available materials and tools are used, and the populace benefit in the long term from learning about simple machines such as improvised pulleys. These are skills they can use again in the future – and, with luck, they will remember where they learned them.

Other skills are sometimes brought into play. Administrative and logistical skills can benefit

An Army medic checks a Pushtun tribesman's blood pressure. Medical personnel can deliver obvious and immediate benefits to the communities they work with, generating goodwill for the security forces.

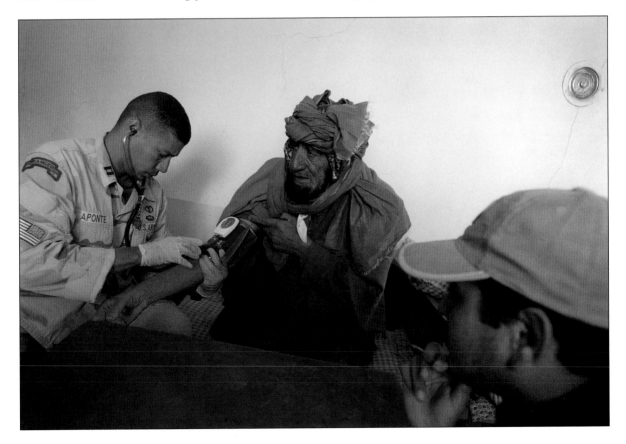

local projects; education skills can be used to teach the locals everything from how better to preserve food from spoilage to how to repair vehicles. Literacy may or may not be of value. If it is, the soldiers may find themselves teaching in an improvised school.

Where possible, the Special Forces team does not simply arrive, 'make things better' and

Hearts and Minds, American style. A Special Forces soldier finds common ground with a group of young Afghan men. This man is fighting the Taliban with a pool cue rather than his H&K submachine-gun, by forming bonds of friendship with the locals.

then move on. All projects are carried out with long-term benefits in mind. If the team seems to be delivering charity, they will make little impression. If they can help the people to help themselves by building confidence and developing their skills, they may be fondly remembered for many years. Years after a deployment, some Special Forces personnel have gone back to the places they served as guests of the people whose babies they delivered – or as guests of those babies, now grown to adulthood.

Sometimes, however, the most useful thing the Special Forces

unit can do is call in help. The locals may have no way to request help or may (perhaps rightly) believe that nobody would respond to a call for aid.

However, if in the opinion of a trusted expert such as a Special Forces team leader the locals need help, something will probably be done.

Normally such a call for aid would be to deal with a disaster or other crises – to prevent famine or disease, or in the immediate aftermath of an earthquake. However, there are other possibilities. For example, in at least one case military lawyers have represented local peasants in

a dispute with landowners. The ability to call in anything from an airstrike to an accountant is a useful function in winning over the population at the 'grass roots' level.

Of course, Special Forces teams are excellent fighting soldiers. They can do much to dispel the myth that the guerrillas have control of the region, that opposing them is dangerous and that the authorities are impotent. For example, snipers may eliminate 'tax collectors' extorting money or supplies from the locals or guerrilla leaders. The team can protect local settlements from threats ranging from guerrilla enforcement units to wild animals.

ANTI-INSURGENCY OPERATIONS

In addition to turning the populace against the insurgents and securing areas against them, it will be necessary to locate and capture or destroy their key personnel. Casualties among the rank and file may be extremely high without breaking the morale of the fighters themselves, simply because, in a highly compartmentalized organization, they may not know how badly things are going. Reports from government sources will be dismissed as propaganda. But if leaders, Party commissioners and the like begin to disappear, then the message will get through and, in the meantime, these individuals will

Special US government instructors from Operational Detachment Alpha (ODA), right, train soldiers from the Afghan Security Guard (ASG) at a Forward Operation Base in Naray, Kunar August 2006, eastern Afghanistan. ODA forces are made up from US military special forces, government intelligence agencies, FBI and specialized law enforcement units.

be unable to exert their influence over their followers.

The most basic Special Forces operation against an insurgency is the patrol. Skill at operating in the prevailing terrain is vital to success here, as the force will have to operate for some time and over a considerable distance. They will be facing enemies who

LEARNING TO HELP THEMSELVES

Perhaps more importantly, Special Forces teams can also help the locals learn to protect themselves from the guerrillas and other threats. Issuing weapons or training people to use them is a powerful gesture of trust, and it can be a two-edged sword. However, once a measure of trust has been generated, it can be the key to breaking the guerrillas' hold on the region. Most insurgencies rely on a mix of sympathy and fear to keep the populace in line. A settlement that is confident enough to defy the guerrillas needs only to become neutral towards them, refusing to provide support and supplies, thus hindering their cause.

If the locals come to realize that they do not need the guerrillas and, indeed, blame them for some of their misfortunes and start to feel that they can defy the insurgents with impunity, then the region will become very hostile for the guerrillas, especially if the Special Forces team can put in place a mechanism for the locals to pass information to the authorities or request assistance.

Measures as simple as providing a mobile phone to a village headman and teaching him how to use it have paid dividends. However, this is only of use if the user feels inclined to call for assistance or to inform on the insurgents, and to a great extent this is dependent on all the measures discussed in this section. Teaching the locals to defend themselves against the guerrillas and giving them the confidence not to live in fear are the final pieces in the 'hearts and minds' puzzle.

When setting up defences for a settlement, there are some general rules that must be followed if the system is to be successful. First, there must be sufficient will on the part of the locals actually to use their defences and not just give in. Second, some kind of mobile support must be available to come to the aid of a fortified village that is under attack. If these criteria are met, then a successful set of defences will follow these principles:

- Defences must cover all approaches.
- The defences should include obstacles such as barbed wire or thorny plants that do not impede the defenders' vision or line of fire.
- Strong points (e.g. earth bunkers) should be mutually supporting and must cover all possible approaches, but especially gates and other passages through the obstacle belt.
- If heavy weapons are deployed, their positions should be concealed and, where possible, varied.
- Observation posts should have a clear, all-round view and be capable of communications with strong points and headquarters.
- Provision should be made for casualty evacuation and treatment, and for the employment of a reserve to back up a threatened sector.
- Food supplies and other materials of use to the insurgents should be located inside the defended perimeter.
- There should be a clear chain of command, a means to raise the alarm and also a way of summoning assistance in the event of a heavy attack.

Of course, when creating local defences the Special Forces team must work with what it has available, and in some cases creating weak defences may be worse than none at all, as this invites attack and defeat, discrediting the project and, implicitly, the authorities on whose behalf it was carried out.

---

might be ill–trained and undisciplined but who have lived in the region all their lives and may be intimately familiar with the ground. To stalk enemy combatants on their own ground takes skill, patience and confidence, but it offers the best chance to strike at the insurgents. There is also one added factor: if the insurgents think that they have a safe haven to retreat to, and are suddenly attacked in it, morale will suffer.

One trick sometimes used by guerrilla forces, which can be turned against them, is the tactic of making an attack to draw a response, then ambushing the relief force. In this case, the operation is carried out the other way around. Special Forces units in the field may be able to warn their regular military counterparts that guerrillas are on the move and perhaps predict the target. Whether or not the attack is a success, the guerrillas can be ambushed as they return to camp, or even in their own camp.

It is sometimes necessary to carry out strikes or raids against settlements known to be harbouring guerrillas. Regular forces with vehicles or heavy support are often rather obvious, allowing the insurgents to slip away before the attack arrives. A Special Forces unit that can infiltrate close to the target gains the advantage of surprise, which can be used in various ways.

The most obvious approach is to make a direct attack by surprise. However, another option is to call in regular forces and observe the guerrillas as they move out of the village or go into hiding. They can then be ambushed as they retreat or return

A US Special Forces corporal leads a file of Tunisian Special Forces along a path during a joint exercise. There is often a feeling of comradeship between the elite forces of different nations. They have similar missions, share the same dangers and usually recognize kindred sprits in their foreign comrades.

after the raid. This approach is more likely to be successful against highly fluid forces that can scatter and regroup at need.

LOCAL VOLUNTEER FORCES

Locally raised forces can be invaluable in defeating guerrillas on their home territory. The

Female Afghan police recruits fire AK-47 assault rifles during target practice at a regional police training centre, June 2006 in Kandahar, Afghanistan. The police receive a 5–9 week training course supervised by American special forces trainers at the centre.

decision to trust locals is a difficult one, and a team that makes the wrong decision may find themselves led into an ambush. On the other hand, failing to give trust where it is due may alienate the populace or, at the very least, result in missed opportunities.

Local volunteers will know the terrain as well as the insurgents. Indeed, they have often been recruited from 'turned' guerrillas who have switched allegiance for all manner of reasons. These units may be deployed as scouts for a Special Forces or regular army operation, but are often trained to operate

independently. They can operate much as the guerrillas do, posing as innocent civilians (or even as guerrillas) while they gather information.

In addition to defending villages and other important places, local irregulars can be used to monitor border regions and other remote areas. They may actively oppose the insurgents or simply report on their movements. In many cases, these indigenous units are recruited from a different ethnic, religious or social group to the insurgents, and may feel threatened by them or have their own scores to settle. Training and equipping these

forces can lead to problems later on if their loyalties shift or if they no longer want to cooperate with the authorities.

This problem can largely be avoided by good liaison and mutual respect built up between the 'indigs' and the Special Forces personnel sent to train and organize them. Much can depend on the actions of a small group of men, very far from home and among strangers.

One historically effective use of locally raised forces is in the creation of 'pseudo-terrorists'. This technique was probably pioneered during the Mau Mau uprising in Kenya. In order to

Iraqi soldiers conducting routine security checks on a car passing their checkpoint. Routine security measures make life difficult for insurgents by restricting their freedom of movement and increasing their chance of being captured.

TUNNEL CLEARANCE

Underground hiding places, often with their entrances concealed under a village, were extensively used in Vietnam. Many different insurgent groups have used tunnels, caves and sewers, and clearing them is a dangerous business. In Vietnam, the troops who specialized in these operations were known as 'tunnel rats'. Generally men of small stature who could fit into small spaces, the tunnel rats were required to wriggle through narrow passages, which might be booby-trapped, in search of caches of arms and supplies, and possibly hidden enemy personnel. Tunnel rats could carry only a handgun and a torch, and operated in a very dangerous environment without any possible support. Even in less restrictive surroundings, penetrating an underground area held by the enemy is a difficult and hazardous undertaking that may be beyond the capabilities of the average soldier. Here, and in many other environments, the Special Forces soldier may be the only way to search and clear the enemy stronghold, going where conventional forces cannot go.

US Marine Lance Cpl Ambakisye-Olutosin Smith, of the Marine Quick Reaction Force, makes his way down into a tunnel which leads to a World War II era bunker near the Somali border to conduct clearing operations, Djibouti, October 2005. The bunkers are seen as possible terrorist insurgency threats and are checked on a routine basis.

penetrate the organization of the insurgents and gain information about them, the authorities used disguised soldiers, 'turned' guerrillas and local volunteers to create 'pseudo-gangs' armed and equipped similarly to the insurgent gangs.

In a highly decentralized insurgency, few of the members will know anyone outside their own small group. When groups meet, it is not 100 per cent possible to know if members of an apparently friendly group are what they seem. The advantages for the authorities are manifold. Most obviously, it is possible to identify enemy leaders, arms suppliers and informants, with a view to arresting them later or setting up an ambush after the meeting.

Discussion of methods and plans will give the authorities either hard and immediately useful information or at least an idea of how the guerrillas operate, their organizational structure and so forth. Even if the guerrillas realize they are being infiltrated, this still benefits the authorities in some ways by reducing trust and cooperation between groups. It is possible that loyal insurgents may be singled out as informers and killed, or that a misunderstanding might lead to combat between groups. Sowing dissent in this way can weaken the insurgency from within.

In some cases, high-ranking members of the insurgency can be 'turned' to become loyal to the authorities. This may be in return for amnesty or if they can be convinced that it is in the interests of their people to surrender. In the Malay Emergency, the insurgents were highly compartmentalized for security reasons. Often, the only contact between many groups was the local Communist Party Commissioner. Some of these individuals were 'turned' and led the authorities to their groups, or else convinced them to come in and surrender. With no other contact between groups, the guerrillas did not realize what was happening to their organization, or who was responsible.

CHAPTER SIX

COUNTER-INSURGENCY WARFARE

Increasingly, modern armed forces find themselves involved in what has become known as 'Operations Other Than War'. Rather than fighting a clear-cut war against a known and easily identified enemy, troops may be detailed to protect refugees or aid workers on 'Operations In Support of Peace'.

One common deployment of this sort is counter-insurgency operations, where the opposing force is not a regular army but a guerrilla or terrorist force. Operations against such opponents may be treated as purely military or may be carried out in conjunction with law enforcement. Counter-insurgency operations are frustrating and complex affairs with many rules of engagement and restrictions placed on the troops involved.

A 12-year-old Karen soldier poses with his US-made assault rifle on the Thai-Burmese border. His comrade, scarcely any older, is armed with an AK assault rifle. While the idea of child soldiers is repugnant to civilized thinking, hundreds of thousands serve in guerrilla and even national armies around the world.

Rebels of the Revolutionary Armed Forces of Colombia (FARC) on parade, 2001. The more successful an insurgency becomes, the more its fighters begin to resemble a regular army – and for this reason, many insurgencies try to seem more legitimate and successful by adopting a formal rank structure and the trappings of a regular force.

group will distance itself from the 'military' arm of the rebellion and pretend legitimacy, though this is not always the case. An overt political group may raise funds and campaign for public support for the insurgency. In other cases, the political leadership may be hidden and play no public role.

In order for there to be any kind of insurrection, there must be at least a measure of public support. This requires a segment of the population to have a grievance against the government or an agenda of some kind. Alliances between political groups are not uncommon. Where possible, the insurgents will try to rally as much popular support as possible for their cause.

THREE STAGES OF SUCCESSFUL INSURGENCY

According to Mao Tse-Tung, who led the ultimately successful insurrection in China, there are three stages to a successful insurgency or guerrilla war. In the first phase the insurgents are relatively weak and must proceed cautiously to build up their strength. They will launch raids to capture weapons and equipment, and seek to create

THE NATURE OF INSURGENCY

Most insurgencies are political in nature. Many involve religion in some way but it is most likely to be used as a political tool by the insurgent leaders. For example, the Taliban in Afghanistan is a Muslim organization, but pro-Taliban terrorists are not terrorists because they are Muslims; they

are terrorists because of the political agenda of the Taliban.

There will always be a political force of some kind at the core of any insurgency. This may be an actual political party or simply a group with an agenda, but in either case it provides the overall direction for the insurrection. Sometimes a political

'safe' areas where they enjoy considerable support. This allows their personnel to rest and train without the constant fear of capture.

As the insurgency gains in strength and proceeds to stage two, the guerrillas begin to take control of more territory, always seeking to discredit the government and demonstrate that it cannot control the country. Some operations are launched with the goal of improving the guerrillas' strength and arsenal, and some to rally public support and undermine the government. All the time the guerrillas aim to increase their strength and gradually create conventional forces capable of defeating the government's army, perhaps in open battle.

Phase three is the 'end-game', in which the insurgents, who by now resemble a conventional army, drive the government forces from critical areas (including the capital) and gain control of the country.

Mao postulated that these three phases might take place at different times in parts of the country. One area might be strongly controlled by a large and powerful force, but the insurgency might still be gaining strength in another region. Setbacks in one area would be compensated by advances

elsewhere. Mao understood that the overall goal was a political not a military one, and was less concerned with defeating government forces than with gaining the support of the populace.

Insurgent forces in phase one and two may be very loosely

organized, and might follow almost any organizational and rank structure that seems appropriate. Formal, quasi-military rank is often used within insurgent organizations to increase the feeling of legitimacy among its members, and as the insurgency progresses towards success, its

A British soldier observes the effects of bombing on a Taliban position. While air assets and artillery can deliver massive firepower, effectiveness requires personnel on the ground to direct the attack and report on its results.

structure tends to become more formalized.

Progressing to stage three too soon can result in defeat by superior government forces. However, it is usually possible to fall back to stage one or two until momentum has been rebuilt. General Giap was forced to do this during his campaign against the French in Indochina. His early attempt to move to stage three was defeated but, after falling back on guerrilla methods, he was ultimately successful.

These Chechen rebel fighters are seen against the backdrop of a burning gas pipeline. Insurgents often try to attack the economy of their target state rather than its military forces.

INSURGENCY STRATEGY

The key to successful insurgency is the support of the people. According to Mao, there are certain precepts that should be followed by all insurgent personnel. Gaining the trust, respect and support of the population was a matter of being seen to be fair, polite and respectful towards the people. Damage done and items taken should be paid for, and returned where appropriate. Damage should be avoided wherever possible, and the people should never be bullied or harassed.

Similarly, Mao urged his personnel to treat captives well so that they might be converted to the cause or at least speak well of

their captors when released. This represents a useful propaganda tool in that released captives might go back to their unit and talk about the decency of the insurgents, countering government propaganda painting them as 'bad guys'.

Mao also recognized that merit and courage among the insurgents should be rewarded. A rank system is an important part of this, along with some kind of system for recognizing those who have done well. Personnel react well to the knowledge that their efforts are noticed and approved of by their superiors, while the feeling that the higher-ups simply do not care how they perform is counterproductive.

THE LONG GAME

The basic strategy and tactics used by successful insurgencies all over the world are remarkably similar. More than anything else, the insurgents know they are playing a long game and are working towards political ends rather than military objectives. This takes the form of increasing control, starting with small rural settlements and gradually moving into the major population centres.

Successful insurgents must make use of the principle of concentrating force at a critical point to achieve their aims and then dispersing again to avoid counterblows. This allows victories over numerically superior numbers. Initially, attacks will be made on easy targets isolated from support. Strikes against better-defended targets will impress the populace more, but a steady stream of minor victories is worth more than a hit-and-miss campaign of spectacular successes and painful defeats.

The aim is to erode the government forces' ability to fight and, just as importantly, the perception of that ability among the general populace. Police posts, tax offices and similar symbols of governmental control are popular targets because they demonstrate the government's inability to control its territory. However, the insurgents do not seek to capture ground and hold it against all comers; that is a certain

A US Army soldier with the 2nd Battalion, 325th Airborne Infantry Regiment, is confronted by smiling children as he participates in the final weapons sweep of Operation Scorpion Sting, June 2003 in Doura, a district of southern Baghdad.

path to defeat. The successful insurgent force attacks at a time and place of its choosing, then melts away again. The same target might be attacked several times in the course of a campaign.

POLITICAL CONSIDERATIONS

The political significance of operations must always be considered. Defeat does not merely cost the lives of personnel and stocks of weaponry; it reduces the standing

Checkpoints and security searches are necessary but much depends on how they are perceived. If the insurgents can convince the population that these forces are oppressive, their cause will gain support.

of the insurgency with the population. Battles of attrition should be avoided, though a campaign of attrition is acceptable in some cases where there is a ready supply of volunteers to take the place of losses. Some targets should not be attacked as this may alienate the population, and the possibility of civilian casualties should be considered when planning.

Most insurgent leaders have no particular problem with civilian casualties so long as the authorities can be blamed for them. Indeed, one common ploy is to try to trigger heavy-handed reprisals and 'government atrocities' that will create martyrs to the insurgents' cause and alienate the populace.

Successful insurgents recognize that government forces are at their most vulnerable when on the move rather than in defended positions, and so try to lure them into ambushes or out into difficult terrain, far from their supports. Every victory needs to be exploited

for its propaganda value and for material gains. If military-grade weapons can be seized from enemy personnel, this will help support future operations. Pressure must also be kept up. If the insurgents are not active, it may seem that the government is winning, and in this kind of campaign perceptions have a way of becoming reality.

ASYMMETRIC WARFARE

'Asymmetry' exists in all kinds of warfare. If it did not, then military operations would proceed like a chess game or else get bogged down in mutual slaughter. By accruing advantages of training,

Vehicle searches are important. This US soldier is using a mirror to inspect the underside of a truck for bombs without touching it or having to actually crawl underneath. Simple tools like this can make the security forces far more efficient.

numbers, weaponry, position, logistics, tactics and so forth, commanders seek to create imbalance in the conflict and thus gain victory. However, the term 'asymmetric warfare' refers to a fairly specific set of circumstances, in which a powerful, technologically superior force is engaged against a low-tech, often irregular, one.

Asymmetric warfare is distinct from terrorism in that it is directed at military targets and is part of a military strategy. However, terrorism is sometimes used in an asymmetric warfare context.

Asymmetric combatants generally have access to very little in the way of advanced weaponry, armoured vehicles, guided weapons or air support. Small arms and explosives, however, are relatively easy to obtain and may be available in large quantities.

One of the big problems facing the asymmetric combatant is that of training personnel. Training facilities tend to be somewhat obvious and vulnerable to strikes by the authorities. Therefore, they are usually small and located in remote areas. Sometimes a country friendly to the insurgents will provide advisors to train personnel, or even allow insurgents to train in its territory. Discouraging this kind of activity is an important part of restricting an insurgency; without outside help, home-grown insurgent forces tend to be less effective.

However restricted the insurgents may be, it is usually possible to conduct small-unit

EXCESSIVE FORCE?

In February 1962, rioting in Georgetown, British Guiana, was so out of control that the police asked for military assistance. The tactic of the time was to form a defensive 'box' formation and move through the affected area under a banner reading 'disperse or we fire'. Warnings to the same effect were given. The tactic worked well enough, and the troops were able to contain the situation and prevent large-scale loss of life.

However, a small patrol at one point came under direct attack by a stone-throwing mob, and the decision was made to fire a single shot in response. The powerful 7.62 round in fact killed three people and wounded another, and questions were raised about the use of excessive force. It is hard to see what else might have been done under the circumstances.

training and small-arms familiarization. This allows small 'cells' to train and work together, more or less independently from one another, a set-up that is also conducive to good security.

This emphasis on small units means that operations are normally small in scale, though several might be coordinated into a larger plan. It will not be possible to defeat the armed forces of a major power using these methods, but that may not be necessary.

'MEANS' AND 'WILL'

There are two components to an effective military force: the 'means' and the 'will'. The means is the hardware and the people who use it, plus the back-up and logistics 'tail' that accompanies all major military forces. This includes everything from rifles and aircraft carriers, and from supply trucks to oil refineries.

Attacking the means can be dangerous – taking on an infantry company in open combat is a hazardous undertaking in the extreme – but the means can be degraded in effectiveness by attacking its 'softer' components. Destroying a tank is dramatic, but cutting off its fuel supply renders it equally impotent.

Asymmetric attacks tend to fall on supply convoys and similar secondary targets, or on isolated and weak units. These tend to be less well guarded and also more vulnerable to the sort of weaponry the insurgents are likely to have available. Attacks make use of surprise gained by concealment or deception, and are rarely aimed at major military assets.

There are, however, exceptions. The attack on USS *Cole* in 2001, using a small boat loaded with explosives, inflicted severe damage on a major combat unit for the cost of two suicide bombers, a small boat and a large amount of explosives. The fact that this was a suicide attack does not mean that this was a 'terrorist' attack – it was a strike on a military unit using unconventional means. Exact repetition is unlikely since measures to prevent such attacks have been put in place, but the general method remains valid and must be guarded against.

Attacks on the means are not ultimately likely to succeed. They are a nuisance, true, and can cause fairly severe problems for isolated units that require resupply through hazardous areas, but this will not win a war for the insurgents.

However, the other dimension, attacks on the will, might indeed bring victory. The most potent

Damage to the USS Cole *put a major naval unit out of action for a long period for little cost. From a military standpoint, the strike achieved little in the long run, but the political effects were considerable. Insurgencies must be fought in the military, political and social arenas if they are to be defeated.*

military force is no use at all if there is no driving will behind it. A demoralized force whose troops do everything they can to avoid combat, or even leave their heavily defended barracks, cannot control the countryside or oppose the insurgents; nor can a force that is restricted by political considerations that have imposed unworkable rules of engagement.

In some cases the deployed personnel and their commanders might be willing to fight but the voting public 'back home' may become opposed to the conflict. This may result in withdrawal, as the government must consider its chances of re-election as well as the nation's interests in fighting the insurgency. This applies mainly to forces deployed

to deal with insurgency in foreign countries or overseas possessions.

Eroding the will of the forces or the public 'back home' requires that the insurgents cause casualties, setbacks and problems for the deployed forces. This of course means attacking the means, but the overall goal here is not the destruction of the means but the collapse of the driving will.

For example, a group of off-duty personnel who are kidnapped and murdered can be replaced with other soldiers, but the attack may affect the will of the government to place its troops in the danger area. A steady dribble of casualties from mortar and rocket attacks, snipers and ambushes may be militarily

A member of the Moro Islamic Liberation Front (MILF) aims a machine gun during a war exercise somewhere in Maguindanao province, southern Philippines, April 2003. The MILF seek to create an independent state in the southern Philippines.

insignificant but can still affect the course of a campaign. It may be that the public (or the troops themselves) may become disenchanted with the whole business, even though the insurgents are not achieving anything worthwhile in a military sense.

Asymmetric attacks are becoming ever more common and inventive, mainly due to the massive capabilities of major power armed forces. At one time,

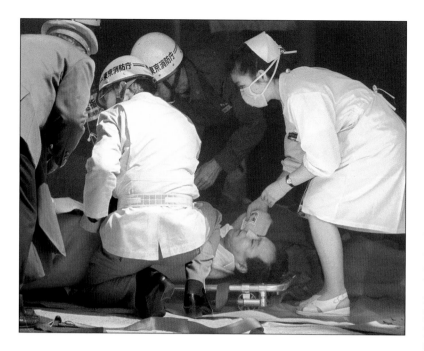

Tokyo medical personnel tend casualties of the 1995 sarin gas attack, which killed 12 people and poisoned thousands of commuters. Most nations now have a response plan in case of a terrorist attack using gas or weapons of mass destruction.

ATTACK ON THE TOKYO UNDERGROUND

Some operations fall somewhere between true asymmetric warfare and outright terrorism. One example is the 1995 attack on the Tokyo underground railways by the Aum Shinrikyo cult. Cult members released sarin nerve gas on underground trains, killing a mercifully small number of people. At the time, the attack looked like simple terrorism.

However, there was more to it than this. The cult was known to be trying to create chemical and biological weapons, and the Tokyo police were conducting special training with protective gear in preparation for a raid on a cult facility.

Realizing that they could not defend their facilities with guns, the cult leaders decided to try to kill as many as possible of the specially trained police personnel by releasing nerve gas on the trains they would be using to get to work, at a time when many officers would be heading in to the stations for a shift change.

Whether this was an act of asymmetric warfare or terrorism is irrelevant; the cult used horrific means to attack its victims in a way that was sure to cause civilian casualties – potentially in large numbers. Whether terrorism or some kind of war crime, such measures are entirely unacceptable to civilized people, and their perpetrators must be fought or imprisoned.

guerrillas who took on regulars in open combat had a realistic chance of winning, but today their chances are not good, so they must be inventive if they wish to survive.

TERRORISM

The saying that 'one man's freedom fighter is another man's terrorist' is not strictly true. Terrorism is the use of fear for a political end, and anyone who does so is a terrorist. This applies to individuals, groups or governments. There have been many terrorist governments in history. Examples include Revolutionary France under the Directory, the Pol Pot regime in Cambodia and the Stalinist Soviet Union.

Purely terrorist groups are different from insurgents as such, in that they intend to get what they want by the use of terror rather than in a military campaign. However, many insurgent groups are willing to use terrorism when it suits them, turning a blind eye or creating justifications for their actions – 'our' terrorists are only using these methods because they are forced to, or because the rightness of our cause permits it, or 'they' did it first, or whatever other justification seems to work.

Terrorists often use economic damage as a tool in their struggle, much as true guerrillas do. The difference is that where a 'military' guerrilla force will try to avoid civilian casualties where possible, much as regular forces do, terrorists do not care or will actively seek to inflict civilian casualties in order to increase fear

among the populace. Terrorists will also strike at military targets even though the military results are not important to them (except perhaps to secure weapons or derail an imminent threat to their organization); the goal is to weaken the will of the government and its forces. Thus, terrorists are as likely to attack the families of troops as the troops themselves.

URBAN AND RURAL INSURGENCY

Government control tends to be easiest in population centres. The armed forces are often based in or close to the main centres of population, and are strongest close to them. Obvious targets such as government installations and police stations have good security and are within easy reach of support. As a general rule, government forces tend to concentrate on the most important urban areas, leaving fewer troops to try to control outlying areas.

The more remote a region, the greater the difficulty of patrolling or even reaching it. This tends to result in a situation where, however much unrest there may be in the cities, the insurgents are more likely to be based in the countryside. As the

Infantry advance through a street with armoured support. Vehicles are vulnerable in urban terrain but their heavy weapons are invaluable at times. The answer is a sophisticated combined-arms doctrine which provides for mutual support and cooperation.

insurgency progresses, gaining control of urban areas becomes a possibility.

Some proponents of revolution and armed insurrection have made a case for the 'domino effect', i.e. the possibility of a successful insurgency in one area triggering another in a different area. While it is certainly encouraging to see like-minded

individuals succeeding (or, at least, not losing), there has to be some unrest to begin with; people do not revolt against the government for the fun of it.

Che Guevara provided one example of this kind of failure. Although he appears on a lot of posters and wrote a lot on the subject of revolution, Guevara's attempt to lead a revolution in Bolivia was spectacularly inept and not a good example of how to do it at all. Guevara seemed to think that success in Cuba would cause the Bolivian peasants to want to revolt. He was killed by the Bolivian army while trying to create an insurrection that had no real popular support. Guevara's big mistake was in assuming that the local people would support and follow him. They had no particular desire to do so, leaving him in unfamiliar terrain without popular support. Having failed to gain the two most basic advantages enjoyed by guerrillas, Guevara was easy to deal with.

The truth is that both urban and rural environments can support insurgency. The key factor is the desire of the people, not the terrain or the environment. However, each environment has its own characteristics.

Compared to urban areas, the countryside is big, and it is difficult to cover all the ground that insurgents might use. Patrolling is the only answer, though it usually means endless hours of hard marching across difficult terrain for no obvious result. Here US troops patrol the mountains near Orgun, Afghanistan.

Insurgent fighters who know the countryside can be very difficult to find, especially in countries with a lot of forest or jungle cover. This camp on the Thai–Burma border is concealed by the surrounding jungle and can easily be moved if compromised.

DISTANCE AND TERRAIN

Distance and difficult terrain work to the rural guerrilla's advantage, along with the fact that security forces are spread thin. Police and military patrols are much more frequent in urban terrain, and response times are much shorter. Rural guerrillas who are discovered or informed on have a better chance of evading capture than their urban counterparts. This is assuming that they are attacked at all; some areas are simply too difficult to get at with the resources at hand. Rural guerrillas may be able to fight off government forces and escape

DEFEATING THE INSURGENTS

Insurgencies can be defeated by the same two factors as government forces – either by the destruction of their means to carry on the struggle, or collapse of their will to carry on. It is also sometimes possible to come to a negotiated settlement, though unless the government decides simply to give the insurgents what they want, their means and/or will must first be eroded until negotiation becomes desirable.

Depending on the type of insurgency, defeat can happen through a combination of factors:

● Removal of popular support.
● Removal of necessary outside support.
● Perception that the insurrection cannot succeed.
● Death or capture of insurgent leaders and personnel.

● Lack of feasible targets or means to carry out operations.
● Offer of an acceptable settlement involving little or no 'loss of face'.

It may theoretically be possible simply to secure everything important and hunker down, and wait for the insurgents to lose heart, but this is not really feasible.

It requires too many personnel, causes too much economic and social disruption and in any event it is not really possible to make attack-proof everything that might be a target. Bunker mentality of this sort is, in reality, a fairly certain route to defeat.

Thus the authorities will need to act against the insurgents, reducing their will to carry on the struggle and their means to do so, and gradually turning the populace against them.

Taliban fighters in Afghanistan. One wears a Russian tank crewman's helmet, perhaps a legacy of the war against the Soviet occupation of the country. Were they met on the street rather than atop an armoured vehicle these men would be indistinguishable from the rest of the population.

notice and with little warning as a result of a tip-off, and an operation (by either side) can be compromised by just one hostile observer with access to a telephone.

All successful insurgencies eventually involve both the countryside and the towns, and in order to defeat one, it is necessary to control both. The first and most important consideration is to ensure that the most critical facilities and areas are well protected. Once essential government and military installations and services are secured it then becomes possible to start operating against the insurgents.

REMOVAL OF SUPPORT

As already noted, some insurrections are supported or even fostered by other nations. Money, weapons and information may be supplied to the guerrillas from overseas, and it is necessary to prevent or minimize this support.

Many nations that support terrorism or revolutionary groups in other countries hide behind a pretence of innocence or polite denial, creating a difficult situation for diplomats trying to convince them to withdraw support. Others admit that 'some

before reinforcements arrive. Urban insurgents are close to military bases and may be overwhelmed by additional troops, or simply besieged until their hideout is assaulted or they are forced to surrender. In the urban environment, the loyalty or, at least, acquiescence of the population is even more vital than in the countryside. Raids can be launched at short

elements' within their country are supporting terrorist groups but wring their metaphorical hands and explain that it is ever so difficult to root them out, for all their willingness to try. This sort of polite fiction has been accepted for many years, but the world is changing. In the wake of the attacks of 11 September 2001, and others since, nations are becoming less tolerant of such quiet support for terrorists.

The invasion of Iraq by the United States and Britain, which toppled Saddam Hussein, was in part a response to a policy of supporting terrorism in Western nations. Not only did the invasion end Iraqi support for terrorism but other nations, notably Syria, also got the message and changed their unspoken policy. Where

such dramatic measures are not possible, the only option is to impose good security measures and try to prevent the flow of arms and money to the insurgent groups.

FUNDING INSURGENCY

Insurgency is an expensive business. It can be made partially self-funding by using captured equipment and engaging in criminal activity such as robbery, drug dealing, protection rackets and the like, but there is usually a source of independent financial backing. In addition to money coming in from other countries (if any), the insurgents often receive money from other benefactors.

Funds can be raised by voluntary donations, and semi-voluntary ones. In the latter case,

people neutral to the insurgency may feel that making a donation to the cause is good insurance. This is more common when the insurgents are doing well in an area, creating a situation where being seen as 'not one of us' can be unhealthy.

If the authorities are seen to be doing a good job of protecting the people and dealing with the insurgents, people may feel more secure and therefore less likely to provide funds, which in turn reduces the power of the insurgency. Other donations come from private sources or

Three US Army National Guard soldiers armed with M4 Carbine rifles react to insurgency small arms fire while on patrol in an Iraqi town during Operation 'Iraqi Freedom'.

British infantry with the support of a Warrior Mechanised Infantry Combat Vehicle on the streets of Basra in 2005. The infantry protect the vehicle and provide all-round observation and the Warrior's gun can deliver powerful support fire if needed.

businesses, often through a legitimate-seeming 'front'. Funding from these sources can be reduced by good implementation of normal civil laws. Routine police investigation of money laundering and membership of proscribed organizations can disrupt the flow of funds to some extent, and of course police intervention in the criminal activities used to fund an insurgency will have the same effect.

However, there are dangers inherent in trying to police insurgent-influenced areas. Drug dealers and bank robbers are often armed, and when they are members of an organized paramilitary force, they may massively outgun the local police. In this case, military support for the police becomes a necessity, and since there is sometimes no way to tell when a 'police' incident may become a clash with armed insurgents, good communications between the police and supporting military forces is a vital necessity.

RULES OF ENGAGEMENT

Some insurgencies are seen as a military emergency and are treated much as any other war.

Prisoners will be taken if possible, but combat troops lead the fight against the insurgents and operations are undertaken in a military context. This means that air power, heavy armoured vehicles and artillery support may be brought to bear on enemy personnel, and operations are undertaken under the direction of military officers.

Other insurgencies are not given 'military' status. In this case, troops are deployed to give aid to the civil authorities and are subject to far more restrictions. Although in both cases there are likely to be strict rules of engagement, in a 'civil' insurrection, the aim is to support law enforcement in making arrests. Captured hostiles are not considered to be prisoners of war. Instead, they are charged with crimes such as possession of explosives or firearms, membership of proscribed organizations or murder.

This has important implications for troops serving against the insurgents. In a military operation they will be much more free to use their weapons, and may be granted permission (or, indeed, expected to) open fire without warning on anyone with a weapon. In an aid to a civil power

This urban sniper can wait for a suitable target, fire, and need not worry about taking return fire. The sound of a shot tends to echo off buildings and can be very difficult to localize, and the small hole is hard to spot. Even if he is spotted, the sniper's sandbags should protect him until he can escape.

situation, troops are expected to issue multiple warnings and attempt to arrest their enemies rather than simply shoot them.

The question of whether the gunman firing at an army patrol is a 'suspect' or an 'enemy combatant' is moot while firing is going on – troops are usually permitted to fire in self-defence or to protect civilians, but it can have implications afterwards.

Rules of engagement exist in most situations outside total warfare, and sometimes even then. For example, British troops operating in the Balkans in the 1990s were often frustrated by the rules that governed them. This led to the absurd situation where snipers were firing through or over British positions but not at the troops occupying them. Since the target

was someone else, the troops were not permitted to deal with the sniper as their rules of engagement only permitted firing in self-defence.

Another example from the same conflict concerns a hostile about to throw a grenade. Troops were permitted to shoot at him until the grenade was thrown, but once it was in the air they were expected to 'detain' the grenadier if they could. A solider who fired after the grenade was thrown (whether or not it had caused casualties) could, in theory, be charged with murder.

There are reasons for rules of engagement, and one of them is the very necessary requirement to avoid giving the enemy propaganda to use after a mistaken (or deliberately provoked) shooting of innocents. However, it can be

very difficult for troops who have just seen innocents killed, or a comrade downed, to see the enemy withdrawing and be unable to do anything about it.

SECURITY MEASURES

Security is vital for the counter-insurgency forces as much as it is for the guerrillas themselves. British forces operating in Northern Ireland faced considerable difficulties in keeping their operations secret from IRA sympathizers among the general population. Something as simple as a sympathizer looking out of

his window and seeing several truckloads leaving the base in the middle of the night will alert the insurgents that something is happening, even if it is not apparent what.

A common trick used by insurgents is to infiltrate spies among the civilian staff employed by the authorities. People with access to a base can read noticeboards, watch traffic and gather a great deal of operational intelligence without doing anything remotely suspicious.

Defeating such infiltration is a combination of deliberate

deception and good house-keeping. Obvious mistakes can be avoided by attention to detail. For example, officers have been known to go to lunch and leave secret documents on their desk or laptops with critical data lying around. Documents should be thoroughly shredded if not needed, and nothing should be left unsecured where it can be read or copied.

Deception measures include assembling transport for a certain time, indicating that a patrol is going out then, but actually sending out the mission several hours before. Similarly, each barracks or base has an area of operations, and enemy observers can be fooled by measures such as sending out a foot patrol as normal, but meeting it in the field with transport from elsewhere and proceeding to an operation in what would normally be another unit's 'patch'.

Routine security measures in the field can interfere with the guerrillas' plans. Something as simple as traffic police stopping a suspicious vehicle can detect an attack or logistic delivery and allow a response to be mounted. Much depends on the vigilance of the security forces or police personnel on the spot.

Just as importantly, good security at potential targets helps deter or defeat attacks, and this helps keep both the means to fight the insurgents and the will to do so intact. Even in the case of people willing to die to carry out an attack, good security and a robust response policy is a deterrent. A bomber may be

A typical team search – one soldier conducts the search while the other covers him from a position where his teammate is neither in the line of fire nor downrange. He also stands where the person being searched cannot easily attack him but can see him with peripheral vision. An armed presence is a good deterrent to violence.

willing to crash a truck loaded with explosives into a barracks if there is a good chance he will kill enemy soldiers, but he is less likely to try if it seems that he will be shot before getting anywhere near. Some people are willing to die to succeed; nobody is prepared to die failing.

CHECKPOINTS AND SEARCHES

One of the most basic tools against insurgents is to restrict their ability to move personnel and equipment around. Establishing checkpoints and searching vehicles or people passing through them is a useful measure if done properly. There is always a risk that ordinary people will resent 'harassment' by the authorities or infringement of their civil liberties.

Resentment can be avoided to a great extent by the conduct of the personnel carrying out searches and manning checkpoints. Different people are predisposed to see them as either jackbooted oppressors or cheerful guardians of society; everyone else will react to their manner and actions.

Checkpoints should always be presented as necessary for public protection, and personnel must be polite and (where appropriate) friendly towards those they stop and search. This must, however, be combined with good control of the situation and care for the safety of comrades.

Iraqi police personnel and soldiers conduct routine vehicle searches in Bulayz, assisted by the US army. Stopping a vehicle can be dangerous; a driver with something to hide may try to run or fight their way through the checkpoint. However, by controlling the roads the authorities limit hostile mobility and activity.

A fairly usual procedure is to have one soldier conduct the search while another is positioned to cover and protect him. Unless there is reason to believe this is a 'hostile' search, i.e. the subject has given reason for suspicion, then roughness or gunpoint searches should be avoided – many residents of Northern Ireland speak of

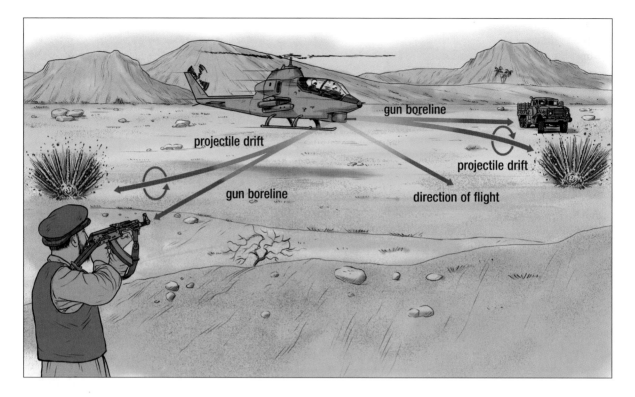

gun boreline

projectile drift

projectile drift

gun boreline

direction of flight

Projectile drift is a phenomenon caused by the fact that bullets spin and therefore wander to the right. They also drop under gravity and both effects are more pronounced the further the projectile must fly to the target. This helicopter gunner must apply a correction to his shots or he will miss the target entirely.

being roughly searched by British soldiers, and considerable resentment was so caused.

One way to maintain control of a search or questioning at a checkpoint is for one soldier to stand not quite behind the subject. He should ensure that he is visible from the corner of the subject's eye as a reminder that he is there, but will not be easily attacked and can intervene if necessary. If a group is being

questioned or searched, then each should be separated from the others in turn, and the group must also be watched.

Checkpoints can be a useful tool for the security forces or an easy target for snipers or insurgent gunmen, depending entirely on the level of training and motivation of the troops manning them. Soldiers need to be confident enough to challenge anything that seems suspicious and to know what to do in any given set of circumstances.

This means that an effective procedure for back-up in the event of attack is necessary, but more than this is needed. Personnel on a checkpoint have to deal with everything from nervous but innocent civilians, through criminals who have

nothing to do with the insurgency, to an actual attack by armed insurgents. Their reactions must be prepared ahead of time. Errors of judgement may be understandable in a split-second situation but their consequences can be severe.

PATROLS AND AMBUSHES

Patrolling has always been an important way to maintain control of an area (and to be seen to be in control) and a means to gather information. Patrols are normally in vehicles or on foot, though in some areas boats are used on waterways.

Patrols offer the insurgents a chance to attack soldiers in the field, attacks made easier by the fact that patrols start at known points (e.g. bases). One ex-paratrooper who served in Northern Ireland always felt most vulnerable when beginning a patrol through a particular doorway onto the street.

The door was thrown open suddenly and everyone rushed out, but the narrow opening allowed only one man through at a time. The first couple to dash out were probably safe enough, but a sniper would have plenty of time to target the narrow doorway as it framed several men in succession. Being one of the last few out of that door was a cause for nervousness. Once out and able to move freely, the soldier felt much better.

British troops patrolling urban areas quickly discovered the value of taking cover whenever possible, and of moving irregularly from one position to another. Even on the streets of a British city, troops needed to use their combat skills to avoid becoming an easy target for a concealed sniper.

Patrols, however vulnerable, are necessary. Apart from being a visible reminder that the authorities are powerful and in control, they allow routine security procedures to be carried out. Suspect persons can be questioned, and unusual happenings investigated. Without a presence in the area, the authorities would never know what was going on there, and without timely information about what is happening in the countryside and towns, there is no chance to deal with an insurgency. Ambushes and counter-ambush tactics are dealt elsewhere in this book and do not need repeating here. It is worth noting how well-trained troops will react differently from irregulars to an ambush, however well motivated the irregulars are.

COUNTER-AMBUSH DRILLS

Regular armies train in counter-ambush drills as well as ways to avoid being ambushed. If an army patrol comes under sudden fire, its personnel know what to do,

In an ambush situation good training really pays off. Instead of creating a chaotic situation, the ambush triggers a well-drilled response as endangered troops seek cover while their comrades cover them, then begin to counter-attack and gain control of the situation.

US forces undertaking a cordon and sweep operation. After sealing an area, troops search dwellings and other buildings for anyone or anything hidden there. There is nothing to stop hostiles moving back in afterwards, except the cooperation of the locals and perhaps the fear of another search.

and also that they can rely on one another for support. Some forces use the Drake drill, responding to unseen ambushers by putting a few rounds into each piece of cover an ambusher may be using. This may disable hostiles or at least suppress them, but it only works if everyone covers his sector and avoids wild shooting. 'Fratricide' is easy in a stressful situation.

Whatever the actual drill used, a properly trained military unit will respond far more effectively to ambush than irregulars. Anyone can shoot from cover by surprise, and usually with a good degree of effectiveness. However, the real quality of a force can be seen in how it reacts when things are going against it.

If possible, a patrol will respond aggressively to an ambush, suppressing the enemy while elements of the force move into better positions, then eliminating the attackers. This is a standard, well-drilled tactic. In a crisis, people react according to their training. Those without any training can usually come up with something on the fly, but it will be

far less effective than the 'each man knows what to do and is confident that the others do too' response of a regular force.

Irregulars who find themselves ambushed, or who are getting the worst of an exchange, are more likely to respond in a disjointed and ineffective manner. Some will hold their ground while others try to escape. Personnel used to working together may be able to coordinate their efforts or, at least, predict what the others might do, but for the most part irregulars will suffer far more from the dislocation and confusion of a firefight that they may be losing.

This trait can be exploited, for example by setting up a one-sided ambush with a clear line of retreat into cover. When the ambush is opened, the insurgents are likely to try to escape in the direction that fire is not coming from. If this area has been booby-trapped by claymore mines and other anti-personnel weapons, the insurgents will flee into a deathtrap.

The trained habits of professional soldiers are designed to avoid disaster or minimize the danger from ambush. For example, even on routine journeys on the roads of the British mainland, army vehicles maintain good spacing and convoy discipline. Were the convoy to be attacked, vehicles following behind would have time to react to the wreck in front of them. This contrasts

with the habits of civilian traffic: many people drive too close to other vehicles and may be unable to react to normal road hazards, never mind the vehicle in front exploding and a deluge of small-arms fire.

This is the key difference between professionals and most irregulars: habits built in good training make regulars a harder target and increase the chances of a successful response.

CORDON AND SWEEP

One tactic that has worked well in some areas is 'cordon and sweep'. Essentially, an area is surrounded by troops, and access to and from it is restricted. Squads then move into the area and begin a systematic search of

possible hiding places. They may uncover arms caches, locate insurgent facilities or provoke a battle with guerrillas who are trying to get out of the area or defend themselves. A mobile force, possibly with armoured vehicles in support, can then swoop on the combatants and arrest the survivors.

Effective sweeps need good coordination between troops and

A cordon and sweep operation in Chechnya. These men, all of military age, have been caught without identification documents during a search. They are confined and guarded until they can be properly investigated. Some or all will be innocent, but the sweep might net hostiles who can then be arrested.

also familiarity with the kind of terrain in which they are operating. Troops unfamiliar with their environment are likely to miss potential hiding places or run into natural hazards, and may leave gaps in the cordon for more skilled locals to slip through.

Cordon and sweep operations can be used in urban terrain, though the multitude of escape routes available makes this a more difficult operation. Sweeps in the towns can also play into the insurgents' hands by alienating the populace, and tend to involve large amounts of time wasted dealing with irate local residents who seem determined to give the troops a hard time for intruding into their business.

Sweeps can net quantities of equipment as well as prisoners, and can force the insurgents to fight on terms not of their choosing. Good operational security is vital, as forewarning will usually lead to the sweep finding nothing.

Effective sweeps can not only clear an area, but also serve as a graphic reminder to the insurgents that they are not safe and so reassure the populace that the government is taking effective measures. The morale benefit of a successful sweep (or even a poor one, if properly presented) can be considerable, and may outweigh the value of enemy personnel captured or killed.

AIR AND ARTILLERY SUPPORT

Air and artillery support can normally only be used against large-scale rural insurgencies, though with the advent of

CORDON AND SWEEP IN ACTION

In July 1952, British troops received information that a terrorist leader was located in the Kuala Langat swamp in Selangor, Malaysia (Malaya). Local police, guard units and British troops cordoned off the area, and search teams were sent into the swamp to find the terrorists.

The search took six days, but eventually contact was made with a party containing terrorist leader Liew Kon Kim. Fire was exchanged and the insurgents fled. The troops gave chase, led by Second Lieutenant Hands, and after an exhausting pursuit Hands personally engaged an armed terrorist and killed him with a submachine-gun burst. The dead terrorist was Liew Kon Kim himself, leader of the infamous Kajan gang. Lieutenant Hands was a National Serviceman, a conscript soldier. His success demonstrates that elite forces are not the only ones who can get results.

precision-guided weapons it has become more practical to deploy heavy weapons.

Air attack, especially by helicopters, can be used to eliminate enemy positions in difficult country where it can be hard even to get troops into the vicinity. Shelling or missile attacks can also be used to make positions untenable. This can be important where insurgent snipers have a good position accessible to them, say overlooking a base. It is not usually possible to garrison all such positions (nor is it desirable in most cases to disperse troops like this), but the position needs to be denied to the enemy. One answer is to pre-register artillery or rockets onto the position and drop some ordnance on it from time to time.

Harassing fire of this sort can be used to deny or impede the use of enemy supply routes. Obviously, this works best where routes run through restricted terrain and are therefore fairly

predictable. Mountain roads and jungle paths are good candidates for harassing fire, though the effect tends to be more of a nuisance than a serous menace to the enemy.

Harassing fire like this has been used to block an enemy's line of retreat. The British in Malaysia often used a technique of shelling the likely line of retreat used by hostiles after a clash. Enemy personnel trying to exit the combat zone were forced to run a gauntlet of shellfire and airstrikes. Even if they could not be precisely targeted in the jungle, the effects were unpleasant and produced a few casualties along with a drain on morale – knowing that making an attack means being shelled on the way home is a demotivating factor.

More precise strikes can be used as a means of eliminating enemy leaders or their head-quarters. This technique has been attempted several times by Israeli forces. One reason for their lack of success is the restraint involved. Rather than use a full-power warhead in their missiles, the Israelis have several times used small warheads in the hope of eliminating the target without collateral casualties. Smaller warheads require a direct hit, which can be difficult to achieve.

Air and artillery support can also be used to rescue a government force that has got into trouble. A classic example is the battle of Marbat in Dhofar, which occurred in 1972. A handful of SAS soldiers were deployed at Marbat to help train local forces who were dealing with an insurgency. About 65 locals and 10 SAS men, who had access to small arms, mortars and some machine-guns plus an elderly artillery piece, defended the settlement.

The defenders were massively outnumbered and outgunned by the guerrilla force that attacked them. Numbering over 250, and reinforced during the battle, the guerrillas had assault rifles, machine-guns, rocket-propelled grenades and numerous mortars.

The defence of Marbat was a heroic affair in which wounded defenders continued to serve the artillery piece, firing at point-blank range into the attackers. As matters went beyond merely desperate, a pair of Strikemaster jets from the Sultan of Oman's air force came in at 15m (50ft), just under the extremely low clouds and at tremendous risk to themselves, and attacked the rebels vigorously. This bought enough time for SAS reinforcements to reach Marbat by helicopter, and the situation was eventually brought under control.

Life goes on. Amid the wreckage of buildings destroyed by Israeli air attacks, the people of Beirut go about their business as best they can. Wrongly directed, air and artillery can alienate the non-combatant population by causing civilian casualties.

Even in the difficult conditions of a sandstorm, US troops remain alert as they patrol Al-Kifl. Bad weather is often used by insurgents to cover movements or even attacks.

existing and new information into a briefing, formulate a plan of action and implement it, all within the shortest possible time frame. Everyone must know his job and be capable of dealing with problems using initiative and either patience or aggression, as appropriate. Given the common insurgents' trick of creating a need for reinforcements somewhere, then ambushing the response force, speed and caution must be balanced by the commander on the spot.

Response forces play an important part in reducing the will as well as the means of the insurgents. The knowledge that an attack will result in fast, effective reinforcement, or that the insurgents can expect aggressive counter-attacks and pursuit drains morale and reduces confidence in success. As already noted, few combatants will embark on a mission that they are sure is going to fail. For this reason, the very existence of mobile forces and a demonstrated policy of effective reinforcement and countermeasures is a powerful tool in the hands of the defenders.

The British in Malaysia used a novel approach to the use of response forces. It proved very difficult to detect enemy forces moving through the jungle to make an attack. Rather than try to guess routes and destinations in order to pre-position an ambush or reinforce the target, the British sometimes chose to rely on good defences at the intended target and transported the response force behind the

The defeat at Marbat discredited and disheartened the insurgents, and played an important part on the road to victory. It owed a lot to the courage and skill of the SAS soldiers and their local allies, and also to the ability of regular forces with good communications to call in effective support when needed.

RESPONSE AND RESCUE FORCES

Mobile forces are an essential ingredient in a counter-insurgency operation. Able to reinforce endangered comrades, pursue retreating enemies and get into new positions quickly, response forces offer the government's officers an extra set of options.

Effective mobile forces need adequate support in the form of bases, logistics and maintenance, and also effective communications with the rest of the deployed forces. This means more than simply having enough radios available. Effective response forces must be able to receive a request for assistance or a deployment order, organize a mission and get to the required point quickly, but without running into trouble along the way.

This requires good liaison protocols, the ability to turn

attackers using helicopters. After the attack, the tired insurgents, often with casualties and low on ammunition, were ambushed on the way back to base or deflected from their path. At best, this was a hammer blow against enemies who thought the battle was over. Even when the ambush failed or the intended victims did not encounter it, the tactic made the journey home longer and more hazardous, and increased the drain on energy and morale by creating a situation in which the insurgents had to remain alert and cautious all the way to their bases.

In some ways, this tactic turned the insurgents' own measures against them. Guerrillas normally feel that they can strike where they will and then slip away, and that this is an advantage over the rather obvious and somewhat static government forces. In Malaysia, the tables were turned. Now it was the guerrillas' turn to wonder if they would be ambushed when they left their bases. Their feelings of security were seriously undermined and this produced a useful morale effect even when dramatic results were not obtained.

CONCLUSIONS

Defeating an insurgency cannot be done overnight. There is always an ebb and flow of advantage in one area and disadvantage in another. Just as the insurgents must move through the three phases to dominance if they wish to obtain victory, so the authorities must push them back the other way.

Counter-insurgency warfare is a draining and frustrating business for the troops involved but, in the end, their conduct is the key. Long hours on guard at

US troops search a mountain cave in Afghanistan for Taliban weapons caches. Most such searches find nothing, but there is always the chance of denying a big weapons cache to the enemy. Unfortunately there is also the chance of encountering enemy personnel willing to fight to protect their armoury.

MOBILE SECURITY

Soviet forces in Afghanistan were required to move convoys of troops and supplies through mountainous areas, along winding roads overlooked by countless ambush points. Some of the best spots were part of local tradition and had been used to ambush local enemies and foreign troops for centuries.

One Soviet solution was to 'leapfrog' airmobile units into position along the heights to guard a convoy as it passed, then move them on to the next objective. Ground vehicles were also used to occupy the more accessible positions, allowing a fast response or, better, denying hostiles the opportunity to

ambush the convoy at all. This kind of operation is very manpower intensive and comes at a high price in maintenance and logistics requirements. Even if there is no ambush, the defenders must use up resources that could better be employed in offensive operations against the insurgents.

A US Army convoy in Iraq. Organised forces require a large amount of logistics 'tail' and this provides a tempting target for the insurgents. An attack will damage the security forces militarily and politically, and may also net the insurgents supplies of weapons, ammunition and other military necessities.

checkpoints or out on patrol can dull the senses, and the tension of knowing that an attack might occur at any time is both tiring and annoying. Yet if an incident occurs, the soldiers involved must spot the problem in time and react quickly, effectively but not excessively.

Insurgents often try to provoke overreaction on the part of government forces, and it is hard to see how a young person who is possibly alone in the dark, cold, hungry and under fire, or faced with the threat of attack, can possibly react in just the right way. And yet, somehow, they do.

A British soldier on patrol in Basra, southern Iraq. The ultimate weapon system. Even in an age of airborne lasers, ballistic missiles and heavy armoured vehicles, the soldier and his personal weapon remain the only indispensable piece of military equipment.

The ability to assess a situation and react with precise ferocity or make a no-shoot decision at the right moment is as much a part of good military training as marksmanship or the ability to dig a defensive position. In today's world, armed insurrection is vastly more common than clear-cut 'war fighting' situations, and while soldiers must always be able to fight battles and win them, they must also be able to defeat the insurgents, the gunmen and the guerrillas.

To do this, they must be able to shoot and fight, but also more than this. They must know how to function as a police officer, rescue worker, firefighter, aid worker, stress counsellor, vehicle mechanic, social worker, friend, neighbour and government official. They must know when to fight, when to hold fire and when to call for help. The days of handing a man a rifle, and simply teaching him how to march and shoot with it, are long gone.

Some may wonder what all these other factors have to do with fighting, but by doing these things as needed, the soldier is indeed fighting a war – he is playing his part in defeating the insurgents, who by their very nature cannot simply be brought to decisive battle and smashed. To be successful, insurgency needs the support of the people. By being seen to protect the community, upholding the rule of law and demonstrating that the authorities are dealing with the problem, the soldier is depriving the guerrillas of that support.

He is fighting the war against the insurgents in the hearts and minds of the people, which is the only place it can be won. And if, somewhere along the way, he must engage in combat with his enemies, so be it. Soldiers tend to be pretty good at fighting.

INDEX

Page numbers in *italics* refer to illustrations.